JOHN DEERE
TRACTORS
THE FIRST GENERATION OF POWER

Holly L. Bollinger

First published in 2004 by Motorbooks International, an imprint of
MBI Publishing Company, Galtier Plaza, Suite 200, 380 Jackson
Street, St. Paul, MN 55101-3885 USA

Motorbooks International titles are also available at discounts in bulk
quantity for industrial or sales-promotional use. For details write to
Special Sales Manager at Motorbooks International Wholesalers &
Distributors, Galtier Plaza, Suite 200, 380 Jackson Street, St. Paul,
MN 55101-3885 USA.

ISBN 0-7603-1753-4

Edited by Leah Noel
Layout by LeAnn Kuhlmann

Printed in Hong Kong

On the front cover: Versatility. That's what farmers wanted from
their tractors by the end of the 1920s. Deere & Company responded
to farmer demand, and to the success of International Harvester's
popular Farmall tractor, with a "general purpose" tractor of its
own—the GP. By 1928, the newly redesigned two-cylinder
tractor began to catch on—enough so that different variations
were made, including this GPO-X, an experimental orchard version
produced in 1930.

On the frontispiece: A lineup of Lindeman tractors. These John
Deere models, based upon the GP tractors, were produced with
crawler tracks instead of wheels so that orchard growers in the
Northwest could travel through loose sandy soil more easily.

On the title page: Singing a higher-pitched "pop" song from its
smaller, faster engine, the Model B, which had 16 variations and styled
and unstyled versions, was the single most popular two-cylinder John
Deere ever sold. The BNH unit pictured here was built midway
through the model's lifespan; its styled face makes for a strong
silhouette on this hillside. Deere & Company made its second round
of Bs a little bigger than the first, giving the popular tractors a
4.5x5.5-inch engine and adding more than 5 inches to their length.

On the acknowledgments page: An Illinois farmer uses a John
Deere–branded walking plow to loosen the soil before planting.
Deere's steel plow, crafted in 1837, was a true agricultural innovation
and launched his career in the farm implement business. By the time
tractors became a part of the Deere & Company line, the company
was being run by a third-generation Deere—William Butterworth,
who was Charles Deere's son-in-law. Charles was John Deere's son and
became the president of the company after his father's death in 1886.
Deere & Company Archives

On the back cover, top: If you were a farmer in 1956, this would be
the working view over the hood of your new Model 420. It's a view
some 46,450 farmers shared. This is the high-crop variation, though
there were general purpose, standard, and other variants. **Bottom:** The
beautiful paint scheme Deere selected for its tractors got the tractors
noticed and admired by the market the company needed to reach. This
colorfully restored 1929 GP pulls a Model 301 three-row planter.

About the Author
Holly L. Bollinger has been writing about the world of agriculture for
more than 10 years now. In that time, she has worked for several ag
industry trade magazines and Web sites as an editor and reporter,
including managing publications such as *Crop Decisions*, *Dealer
PROGRESS*, and *PrecisionAg Illustrated*. Her articles also have appeared
in *Ag Retailer* and *Missouri Ruralist* magazines. Today she is a Missouri-
based freelance agricultural writer and editor with a continuing special
interest in natural resource conservation and high-technology farming.

CONTENTS

ACKNOWLEDGMENTS

My sincere acknowledgments go to all those who pointed me in the right direction and who shared their insights along the way.

I especially would like to thank Mike Kraemer, with the North American Equipment Dealers Association, for his professional consideration and ability to recognize potential. I'm always grateful to my good friend and colleague Bob Wanzel for his years of mentoring and for providing me with many unmatchable life experiences in agriculture. And Andy Markwart at *The Furrow* hooked me up with just the right folks from Deere & Company.

My sincerest thanks go to the especially forthcoming and knowledgeable Neil Dahlstrom. A Deere & Company archivist by trade, Neil also is a talented writer and true historian in many Deere ways. In addition, I've had access to the greatest resource any author could have available—my proficient MBI editors, Leah Cochenet Noel and Lee Klancher, are both dedicated and down-to-earth.

To my family and friends who have offered their encouragement and enthusiasm (and many hours of babysitting)—making it possible for me to pour myself into this chronicle of our not-so-distant agricultural past and the rise of the green-and-gold icons that may very well rule American farm life forever—thank you.

DEDICATION

To my youngest nephew, Brett Travis, whose appreciation for farm life and unadulterated awe of John Deere tractors implies wisdom way beyond his years.

BREAKING GROUND

Horses of a Different Color

"Big iron" was a concept that didn't apply much to agricultural production in the late 1800s. In this pre-Industrial Revolution world, farmers had plows and threshers, but not much more. They were still using handheld tools, as well as teams of horses, which they had used in fields for centuries.

Even though it took nearly 40 hours of labor to produce 100 bushels of corn in 1890, most American farmers trusted

John Deere built his original business on the success of several tentative partnerships. More trusting of associates than his father-in-law, Charles Wiman continued to forge new business bonds after he took over the company in 1859. A decade later, 31-year-old Charles opened a branch house with Alvah Mansur in Kansas City. The collaboration led to the formation of Deere & Mansur Company in Moline, Illinois, in 1877. Popular for its garden tools, the company actually was established to build corn planters; it became a part of Deere & Company in 1909. *Nick Cedar*

these hard labor ways. They didn't trust machines to help them speed their field work because the huge steam-driven tractors were clunky and difficult to operate. Instead, farmers trusted their horses. In fact, the horse was more a part of the farm and farm life than any piece of equipment.

Keeping a team horses, however, meant that farmers had even more mouths to feed. Even a small team of horses consumed at least a few acres each year in return for the heavy work they did. Soon there would be a different way, though, a means of drawing horsepower that didn't eat up its own fruits of labor. It would empower its owner to double his production per hour. And farmers would maintain a dominion over the new beast of burden, which was unmatched in nature.

JOHN DEERE — THE LIFE OF AN IDEALIST
Long before the word "tractor" implied farming, an idea had been seeded in the minds of some that metal-borne power was the future of agriculture. The idea started for one young northeastern blacksmith in 1825. That year ended 21-year-old John Deere's five-year apprenticeship and signaled the beginning of a rocky start to a legendary career.

Soon after striking out on his own, Deere married and opened his own blacksmith shop. But by the mid-1830s, despite solidly crafted products, Deere's business had failed in the local economy, and he left his home state of Vermont.

Disappointed, but not deterred, Deere said goodbye to his young family and headed westward in late 1836 to a small riverside town just days outside of Chicago. He settled his family in Grand Detour, Illinois, and soon began succeeding as a blacksmith in the community made up heavily of transplanted East Coast farmers.

Deere was a great resource to the locals in his visionary understanding of metals and their properties. He also was familiar with the growers' many complaints about how the rich, but sticky, bottomland soils were burdensome to farm. Their main lament was that the traditional cast iron plows from back East clogged easily in the moisture-laden spring fields. Deere realized the solution lay not in the farmers' hands but in the construction of their plows.

One day in 1837, Deere came across a scrap lumber saw blade made of steel while visiting a local sawmill. Somewhere in the reflection of the highly polished metal he saw a revolutionary solution to the farmers' plight. The flexibility of steel would make all the difference in clearing the way for farmers to plant.

Deere asked to have the broken blade, which he then took back to his shop and modified into the first of his many handcrafted implements. The result was a moldboard plow that glided through the thick soil of the Western plains.

By 1842, Deere had plowed his way to success. He even took on a partner and relocated to the industrializing city of Moline. Factory production of Deere & Company's plows was well underway and sales were growing when Deere's son Charles graduated and

A smithy by trade, John Deere made the first steel plow in 1837. This reproduction shows the result of cutting and chiseling a broken lumber saw blade given away by his friend, Grand Detour's prominent citizen and sawmill owner Leonard Andrus. If the steel plow didn't gum up in the heavy black bottomland soils around Illinois' Rock River, it could work anywhere. And it did. By 1939 Deere built 10 more of the same plows, thereby launching his career. *Deere & Company Archives*

came to work for the company. Charles' business and accounting education proved to be a good sales aid in the field when he aptly engaged farmers in conversations about their operations and equipment needs. And Charles followed in his father's footsteps of ingenuity, as he even excelled in the role of new product demonstrator for the company before becoming its vice president in 1857.

As Deere & Company began to branch across the Midwest, Charles expanded his leadership within the company until he took over as president upon John Deere's death in 1886. Within the decade, Charles Deere was already squaring off with the competition, namely the McCormick harvesting empire, a large company headquartered in Chicago.

McCormick banded together with four other large harvester companies in 1902. The resultant mega-company, the International Harvester Company (IHC), soon would be building what Deere was not—tractors.

Charles was very much an idealist like his father. But it would take more than ideas to claim a place in the tractor business. Even without tractor aspirations of his own, Charles Deere tenaciously led the company, decade after decade, as it grew into a leading manufacturer and distributor of steel plows, cultivators, corn and cotton planters, and other implements. At the end of his tenure, Charles successfully staved off roundabout buyout attempts by IHC. But the stress of the constant business battles took a toll on him. In fact, it was said to have cost Deere his life.

After the younger Deere's death in 1907, his son-in-law William Butterworth took over the company reins. Butterworth, a lawyer, was both intelligent and intuitive. He knew that in order to thrive the company would need innovative machines that could solve the problems of producers in every type of soil, climate, and topography. Despite his vision for the company, Butterworth wouldn't have believed that he would one day help build the number one powerhouse of farm equipment. And he couldn't have known that future of American farm power was destined not to be written in black and white—but in John Deere green.

John Deere had a deep affinity for making metal solutions to others', especially farmers', problems. As soon as his 21-year-old son was able to manage the company, Deere—in his early 50s—semi-retired and concentrated full time on tinkering with his products. But his commitment to farmers was already the bedrock of Deere & Company, as evidenced later by corporate literature designed to edify the best use of its plows in 1915 and 1919. *Nick Cedar*

Chapter 1

DAIN, DEERE, AND EARLY TRACTORS

Tapping Into Waterloo

By 1912, more than 200 tractor manufacturers were in business, including the giants, International Harvester Company and J. I. Case. Among those up-and-coming manufacturers was Deere & Company. Already 50 years old and being run by its third generation, Charles Deere's son-in-law, William Butterworth, the company had a solid reputation for building field implements, not tractors.

In light of the competition continuing to push forward in developing tractors, Deere & Company's executive team charged in-house engineer, C. H. Melvin, with creating a prototype for a multi-function tractor.

Previous pages

The Waterloo Boy Model N holds a special distinction as the first tractor put through the Nebraska Tractor Test. Apart from its attractive paint and lettering, this 1917 model is pure function. From this angle, it looks much like a stationary engine set on axles.

Butterworth knew that the challenge of the day was to build an affordable, dependable, field-ready tractor for the average grower. The typical turn-of-the-century farmer didn't have the money or manpower resources to invest in buying and learning how to run a newfangled iron horse, especially not an unproven one.

Of the few experienced and successful tractor manufacturers, International Harvester was the acknowledged leader.

So Butterworth didn't see a need for Deere & Company to jump headfirst into the risky tractor market. In fact, he didn't approve even experimentation with a Deere-branded tractor plow until mid-1912.

Butterworth certainly wasn't encouraged by Melvin's prototype, which was a failure in most regards. The tricycle configuration required the farmer to sit at the extreme rear of the tractor for plowing, with the two wheels leading. For drawbar applications, the operator switched directions and sat toward the front, just behind the leading single wheel. In the either setup, the design was weak and unreliable.

For such a flop, the development and testing of the prototype was expensive—costing Deere & Company nearly $7,000. Consequently, Butterworth perceived the full-scale development of a general-purpose farm tractor as daunting—

John Froelich created the first known self-propelled gasoline tractor in 1892 with this machine that used an engine from the Van Duzen Gas and Gasoline Company of Cincinnati, Ohio. That same year, Froelich used a successful trial of the tractor to form the Waterloo Gasoline Traction Engine Company with the support of several Iowa businessmen. The company became the forerunner to Deere & Company's tractor venture. *Deere & Company Archives*

it was a challenge that could potentially ruin Deere & Company if not met adequately. After all, some of Deere's top competitors, among them Rumely, Emerson, and Hart-Parr, were destroyed in a single season when poor agricultural conditions compounded failed investments in tractors.

In 1914, Deere & Company vice president, Joseph Dain Sr., latched onto the board of directors' invitation for him to investigate a plausible tractor design. Dain had joined Deere & Company four years earlier, when it bought his company, Dain Manufacturing based out of Ottumwa, Iowa. The minutes from that fateful board meeting read: "Mr. Dain was asked to report to the Executive Committee whether or not a tractor could be built to sell at about $700 and in the meantime to suspend work of development until his report is made."

A few months later, having been convinced by Dain, the board concluded in session: "June 24, 1914. Resolved: That the preliminary work of designing an efficient small plow tractor be continued under the auspices of Mr. Dain and the Experimental Department."

While the board approved Dain's new project, Deere & Company's leader was extremely hesitant to acquire a reputation as a tractor manufacturer. Butterworth spent much of his time using his clout to assure others, mostly investors, that Deere & Company was never going to be in the business of making tractors. But Deere branch managers were complaining that they were losing sales because they, unlike other farm equipment suppliers, had only equine-fitted plows to offer. The result of Dain's efforts, in 1915, was the first line of Deere tractors, although internally they were always called Dain's.

Dain's first two prototypes were reverse tricycle-style iron workhorses, weighing more than two tons each and pulling upward of 3,000 pounds in field tests. But it was Dain's third effort that got John Deere's company into the tractor manufacturing business.

At the March 14, 1916, board of directors' meeting, Dain's third version, proven successful in Texas tractor trials, convinced board members to make this decision: "Resolved: That Mr. Dain be requested to reconstruct said tractor with such modifications as may be deemed wise by him and his associates, preparatory to economical manufacturing."

The board ordered about 10 machines into production, which meant that one of Deere's operating plants would have to be retooled. The John Deere Spreader Works Marseilles plant in East Moline, Illinois, became the first Deere tractor factory, and the Dain All-Wheel Drive development models that came out during the next year were notably different from competing tractors. The multi-chain drive system was an improvement over single sprockets and chains and was more durable than gears. Chains also were easier for farmers to adjust and repair.

The quality materials used in the Dain four-cylinder tractor made it likely to retail for $1,200. Deere executives, still skeptical that farmers would pay so much for such a lightweight model, agreed making the tractor dependable was the number one priority.

A written recommendation to the board by George Schutz, Deere & Webber's Minneapolis branch manager, expressed the magnitude of manufacturing a quality product: "Our tractor should be strong enough and have power enough to pull three-bottoms in stubble, under almost any condition, as the majority of farmers when purchasing a three-plow tractor expect it to do better and deeper plowing than they could with horses. A good many tractors are sold at times when plowing conditions are unusually hard for horses."

After weighing the benefits of a well-made tractor to the heavier competition, Schutz concluded enthusiastically, "In considering the matter of price we must remember the more tractors we sell the more tractor plows we will sell!"

By 1917, Dain and Schutz, working together, had redesigned the Dain tractor to include a stronger McVicker vertical four-cylinder gasoline engine, ball and roller bearings to improve drivetrain problems, heavier drive chains, and a new gear transmission that ran submerged in oil for increased cooling and lubrication. The success of this overhaul sent Dain's seventh model into Deere's first mass tractor production for the next year.

Unfortunately, Dain never saw the first of the hundred of his redesigned tractors built by Deere. On October 31, 1917, seven years from the day he joined Deere & Company, he died of pneumonia complications in a Minneapolis hospital.

Knowing that the first line would be ready to ship by June 1918, the board began planning for the next phase of production tractors. For this, they needed a major tractor production facility—the Marseilles works was not large enough.

The search for a production plant didn't go far beyond Deere's hometown. In Waterloo, Iowa, little more than 100 miles west of Moline, the executives found exactly what they were looking for—and much more. The Waterloo Gasoline Engine Company not only had the land and factory Deere & Company needed, the company had a working, selling tractor line of its own in the Waterloo Boys.

THE WATERLOO BOY GOES TO WORK FOR DEERE

Before the idea of tractor mechanics caught on, John Froelich believed he could create such a machine. Froelich was a traveling thresherman who made his way by harvesting the vast expanses of wheat fields across the Great Plains. In the late summer of 1892, he brought an experimental vertical one-cylinder, self-propelled, gasoline-burning tractor to

NEBRASKA TEST No. 1 (1920)	
Tractor model	Waterloo Boy N (bought by Deere & Company in 1918)
Production years	1917–1924
Serial numbers	8378–31412*
Drawbar rating (hp)	12
Belt pulley/PTO rating (hp)	25
Fuel	kerosene (run)/gasoline (start)

The Waterloo Boy N was the first tractor ever tested at the Nebraska testing laboratory established in 1920.

Note: The serial numbers listed in these tables occasionally include overlapping and isolated production numbers from separate tractor models, and therefore should be not be considered as fixed, serialized number spans but instead as all-inclusive guidelines to accompany the tractor models and their years of production.

Through 1959, all Nebraska Tests resulted in triplicate ratings: observed horsepower, corrected horsepower, and rated horsepower. First, testers modified the outright "observed" horsepower using a standard equation to adjust the rating for both sea-level barometric pressure and a constant temperature of 60 degrees. Then, they multiplied the "corrected" drawbar and belt horsepower numbers by .75 and .85 respectively, which determined the "rated horsepower."

The results of rated horsepower more closely resembled the actual working conditions most farmers would encounter in their fields. Thus, tractor owners would have more realistic expectations from their equipment.

Nebraska Test horsepower ratings that are boxed separately from the main text throughout this book are written according to the "rated horsepower" Nebraska Test results listed in Deere & Company's publication, John Deere Tractors 1918 to 1994.

Plowing and hauling obviously require motive power, but a tractor engine can also serve as a pump or a driver for other machinery. The Type T Portable offered farmers the latter capabilities at a reduced cost when compared to a self-propelled model.

farmlands near Langford, South Dakota, to power his threshing machine. According to U.S. Department of Agriculture records, Froelich designed his contraption by mounting a Van Duzen gasoline engine on Robinson running gear "equipped with a traction arrangement of his own manufacture." This 16-horsepower, four-and-a-half-ton machine was groundbreaking in that it was the first gasoline tractor that propelled itself forward as well as backward. It also had a successful initial trial. During its first 50-day run, Froelich's tractor pulled and powered a thresher over difficult terrain, operating in temperatures from late summer highs near 100 to –3 degrees Fahrenheit in the autumn-frozen hills, eventually threshing more than 72,000 bushels of small grain. The success of Froelich's tractor was short-lived. After forming Waterloo Gasoline Traction Engine Company with a group of Iowa businessmen, Froelich discovered that the tractors he designed could not stand up to long-term farm use and never duplicated the success of his first tractor. By 1896, Froelich had built just four tractors to sell and sold only two—but even those two were returned by disappointed customers. The Froelich tractor's lack of success didn't deter the Waterloo company's other owners from recognizing the value of the engine, which performed well and had a market as a stationary power source. After all, the belt pulley provided plenty of energy to run a thresher.

The profitability of the stationary engine models and Froelich's simultaneous departure in 1895—spurred from frustration over the failure of his tractor design—led the company to drop the word "traction" from its name, thus becoming the Waterloo Gasoline Engine Company. With Froelich gone, Waterloo Gasoline Engine was free to focus on selling its stationary units and portable versions. The latter didn't provide power to wheels but could be loaded on a

Stationary engines, like this 1925 Model W, served the farm by pumping water or generating electricity. The metal runners kept the engine in one place during operation, but facilitated dragging with their turned-up ends.

wagon bed and hauled into fields by a team of draft animals to run other machines, such as threshers, from the belt.

But soon it became clear that the agricultural industry viewed stationary engines as standstill technology because the farmer still needed a team of horses to pull the engine where he needed to use it. To move ahead in the industry, and to get more farmers investing in modern machine movement, the engine power needed to move itself. And competition from budding tractor makers pressured Waterloo Engine to get back into traction.

So the company hired engine designer Louis Witry, a former railroad engineer, and Harry Leavitt, an engineer in the new field of tractor design who had developed roller tracks as an alternative to wheels for "crawler" applications, to create Waterloo's 1913 moving engine, the self-propelled Waterloo Boy One-Man Tractor.

The Witry-Leavitt team continued refining the design of the 9,000-pound original Waterloo Boy over the next few years. With the help of an engine design brought into the company by A. B. Parkhurst from Moline, Illinois, Waterloo released the three-wheeled, one-wheel-drive L and the four-wheeled, two-wheel-drive LA models in 1914. Both the L and LA ran on a two-cylinder, two-cycle kerosene-burning engine design, in which the cylinders were horizontally opposed. At a maximum rpm of 750, this engine design produced a mere 7-horsepower-pull, running at 15 horsepower off the belt.

Later that same year, Waterloo engineers improved the engine by using a horizontal side-by-side cylinder design. The new engine ran through four cycles and produced a distinctive "pop-pop" sound that would ring true to farmers through many years and help build the icon of later John Deere models.

The new engine, mounted on an LA chassis, became the Waterloo Boy Model R tractor.

The Type T, like the Model N, used a detachable cylinder head. The two horizontal cylinders had upright sparkplugs, and long external pushrods acted on vertical rocker arms to open and close the four valves.

This Waterloo Boy Model R is from the first year of production, 1914. Note how far behind the rear axle the driver sits, steering the front wheels through a bolster-and-chain system.

The radiator on early 1915 Waterloo Boy Model Rs, like this one, was mounted longitudinally. In this design, both the fan and the water pump were turned by crank-driven belts. The Model R was the first of the company's tractors to start with gasoline but run on kerosene. Later in the year, the company upped displacement from 330 to 396 cubic inches on Model Rs and switched to a horizontal tank to minimize fuel-flow problems on hills.

Simple geometric shapes comprise this 1915 Waterloo Boy Model R. Its straight lines and simple curves made tooling and manufacturing easier. The three rods that seem to intersect the spokes are braces for the large drive gear.

The tractor had a single forward speed and a bolster-and-chain steering system that pivoted with the angled front axle. It paved the way for future kerosene engines, as it was the company's first of many two-cylinder, gasoline-start and kerosene-run successes. Thirteen styles of the Waterloo Boy Model R, designated RA through RM, sold through 1919. The 14th variation, Model RN, officially became the Model N in 1917.

Waterloo continued experimenting and making small improvements as it continued selling various styles of basically the same tractor during the next five years. The biggest difference among most of the versions was the engine design. Models RA through RD used an integral head and block with 5x7-inch bore and stroke. Variations E and G had an increased size of 6x7 inches. In 1916, the engine was modified to a separate head and block. The H through L models coupled this

design with a 6x7-inch bore and stroke, which engineers increased further in the RM to 6.5x7 inches.

The last of the Waterloo Boys, the Model N, had a unique look, with an immense drive gear that nearly matched the size of its rear wheels. Designers returned to the proven worm-and-sector, automobile-style steering system, used roller bearings in the engine, and incorporated a two-speed transmission—just as other tractor makers of the day had.

The Model N, built through 1924, had an engine with a 6.5x7-inch bore and stroke that provided 12 horsepower to the drawbar and 25 horsepower on the belt pulley, running at 750 rpm. The N was complete tractor package, from its lubrication system to its radiator cooling capabilities. It was, in

The Model R from 1915 had only two speeds, forward and reverse, and the operator had 12 horsepower at the drawbar to get the job done.

part, the mature design of the Model N, honed through the 13 previous R-styles, that attracted Deere & Company executives to the Waterloo product line and factory. So in an effort to distinguish itself among the growing number of tractor companies in the United States, Deere & Company bought the Waterloo Gasoline Engine Company on March 14, 1918, for $2.35 million, and the destiny of American tractors took on a new coat of paint.

WATERLOO BOY WORKS OVERTIME OVERSEAS

With World War I monopolizing both manpower and crop and livestock supplies, Henry "Harry" George Ferguson was looking for a way to produce more food for his isolated island homeland of Ireland and the neighboring countries of England, Wales, and Scotland. Crippled by naval battles, the British shipping industry was losing its ability to supply the needs of its countrymen.

Ferguson was a young entrepreneurial mechanic, inventor, and aviator who knew that tractors could more than make up for farmers' wartime losses of grown laborers and mature horses. So he began selling the American-made Overtime Rs and Overtime Ns, which were in essence repainted Waterloo Boy models R and N.

The Overtime, exported to England for sale out of London, was based on the Model R and Model N Waterloo Boy. This 1916 tractor is an Overtime Model R, produced from 1914 to 1919.

The Overtime Farm Tractor Company, based in the east end of London, imported the Waterloo Boys from the Iowa factory and changed the color scheme from the company's bright, soon-to-be-namesake green, yellow, and red to a more muted Rumely green, Allis Chalmers orange, and light battleship gray pattern.

Throughout Great Britain during "the war to end all wars," the imported Waterloo Boy tractors lived up to their new names as they worked overtime in the fields to feed the British and Irish soldiers and citizens.

Ferguson went on to serve on the Irish Board of Agriculture where he took on the job of teaching farmers how to maximize the benefits of using tractors. Finding few overwhelming benefits in the Overtime's blueprint, Ferguson worked on his own tractor design, creating a revolutionary farm implement hitching system that later would rival Deere & Company's own innovations for decades.

His machine design improvements eventually became the launching ground for Ford-Ferguson's breakneck run as the top tractor-maker of the 1940s.

Overtime models, shipped to England, featured bright orange paint on wheels and other mechanicals. In close-up, the mechanicals resemble those of a wristwatch. The design is good for a top speed of 2.5 miles per hour, whether going forward or in reverse.

An obvious distinction between the N and a Model R is the drive gear and the direction of the teeth. The Model R gear is smaller, engaging the driveshaft with outer teeth, while the big Model N gear engages from within. The Model N also featured two forward speeds, for a top forward speed of 3 miles per hour. The large wooden machine in the back of the photo is a Harris Harvester.

The Waterloo Boy Model N proved very popular, with some 21,392 built over the production years from 1917 to 1924. The Waterloo Boy name dates back to 1896, when the company's stationary engines were frequently used to pump water and is believed to be a play on the phrase "water boy," a youth who delivered water around the farm where needed.

The steering chains attach at the front axle of the Model N through a heavy spring, which absorbs shock from ruts and furrows. Deere gradually switched to automotive-type steering beginning early in 1920. Note the one-way treads in back. Working in conjunction with a mirror-image set on the opposite wheel, they pushed the wheels inward and upward at the start of slippage to help keep the tractor from getting stuck.

Chapter 2

JOHNNY POPPER IS BORN

The D Is for Deere

The purchase of Waterloo made Deere & Company a minor-league player in the tractor industry, and the success of Waterloo Boy Rs and Ns negated the need for further production of the Dain All-Wheel Drive model. Deere also had an unforeseen edge over the competition in that the engineering brainpower behind Waterloo's $900 R and $1,100 N was now hard at work on the next generation of the Waterloo Boys. Witry and Leavitt had already developed experimental models, referred to internally as styles A through D (not to be confused with the former Waterloo company's earlier models RA through RN).

The Model D was Deere & Company's first tractor to have been launched solely as a Deere product. It used nearly the same paint colors as its Waterloo Boy predecessors, a distinct green-and-gold scheme that soon would be as recognizable as the John Deere namesake. This first-run Deere had a left-hand cast-iron steering wheel that was perforated by four slots in each of the four spokes.

These new Waterloo Boys were like eye candy to some Deere executives, who were eager to launch the next big tractor. Designers had slimmed down the body by more than a ton, presenting it on a shorter wheelbase and lower chassis, and reversed the now enclosed horizontal two-cylinder engine. In stark contrast to the physical downsizing, the drawbar now pulled at 22.5 horsepower and belt power was up to 30 horsepower.

At the same time, Deere's sire to its eventual tractor reign, the Model D, was nearing completion with new features the engineers had perfected. The problem with introducing such a top-notch machine was the whopping $1,000 price tag. Although the number of U.S. farms was at its peak of 6.5 million in 1920, the country and its agricultural industry were recovering from World War I. The loss of manpower and resource shortages had hit farmers' pocketbooks hard. Aware of farmers' economic woes, Henry Ford started a price war with International Harvester by continually cutting the cost of his popular tractors. By 1921, Ford's dealers were selling the Fordson for less than $400. For many potential tractor investors, price mattered most. As a result, Deere wasn't quite ready to launch an expensive new machine in such a contentious marketplace.

BUYING INTO THE TRACTOR MARKET

While World War I had meant a loss of labor for American farmers, it also spurred an increase in grain prices. Then, abruptly, demand fell for wartime staple crops, such as corn and wheat. By the end of the 1920s, farmers were faced with few remaining foreign markets, mounting commodity surpluses,

A dream field for a Deere collector: a 1917 Waterloo Model N (right), a 1917 Overtime Model N (center), a 1920 Model N (right, background) and one from the final production year, 1924 (left, foreground). The company raised the height of the fuel tank several times during the course of production.

The tractor craze caught on, early on. Even if they didn't have money to invest in tractor-fitted implements, farmers needed the tractor. This farmer made full use of horsepower for disking with his perfectly good horse-drawn ridge-buster—without the horse, of course. *Deere & Company Archives*

and decreasing land values. The farmer knew that mechanical farm power was significant, but he didn't yet believe that his return on investment would be too.

Even the industry's literati heralded, if cautiously, the coming of the all-purpose farm tractor. In 1927, a committee that included representatives from the American Country Life Association and the Farm Economics Association wrote about modern tractors in a book, *Farm Income and Farm Life*. Fancifully subtitled "Symposium on the Relation of the Social and

Economic Factors in Rural Progress," the book reflected the dominant culture of still-traditional farming methodology:

"While tractors have been an exceedingly expensive tool in the hands of many farmers, it is now becoming obvious that some of them, at least, will soon be perfected to a point where they will greatly increase the efficiency of our larger farmers in most parts of the country.

"We are now in the midst of a revolution in farm methods. Theoretically it is possible for this revolution to reach a point

The frame on this 1918 Model N is bolted together. During 1920, the company shifted to riveted frames. The crankshaft on these tractors featured a hand starter crank on one end and a heavy flywheel on the other.

where for each 100 people living on the farm, in the United States, 400 people can live in the villages, towns, and cities. At the present time, however, there are forces at work which make it seem rather doubtful if the increase in the efficiency of the American farmer will be carried quite that far. . . ."

Although the authors never specified the "forces" they were referring to, they likely were attuned to the conventional farming culture and were therefore speculating on the economic circumstances of post–World War I American agriculture. Their thought also might have been that fewer farmers

so-called tractor companies operating in that decade, the majority didn't offer a product reliable enough to be called a production tractor. Instead of actually increasing a farmer's production, many tractors of the day offered a little additional power to help farmers do their jobs. In the end, machine power still wasn't as reliable as manpower and manual horsepower.

In order to get an edge on the competition, many tractor companies were using unscrupulous means to get ahead. Even Henry Ford had lost the use of his name when a Minneapolis company that employed an engineer named Ford acquired the right to use the Ford name for its tractor. Ultimately, politics decided who would survive among tractor manufacturers when Nebraska legislator Wilmot Crozier had the unpleasant experience of mistakenly buying the knockoff Ford. The tractor gave him nothing but headaches. Crozier abandoned the defective model for a used Rumely that performed beyond his expectations, leaving Crozier in wonderment as to why the other subpar tractor could be legitimately sold alongside such competition.

Crozier enlisted the help of another Nebraska lawmaker and farmer, Charles Warner, as well as L. W. Chase, president of the American Society of Agricultural Engineers and professor at the University of Nebraska, to separate tractor industry goods from garbage. The trio lobbied hard for the Tractor Test Bill, which passed on July 15, 1919. The new Nebraska Tests, named after the originators, would force all tractor makers to submit their machines to standardized evaluation of endurance, horsepower, load capacity, and fuel efficiency. Performances and failures became public record.

Deere's Waterloo Boy Model N won distinction as the first tractor to pass the Nebraska trial in April 1920, sealing Deere's reputation as a credible tractor manufacturer. Under test engineers' scrutiny, the three-ton N manifested 12 horsepower on the drawbar and 25 horsepower from the pulley and produced a maximum drawbar pull of 2,900 pounds; it was certified immediately. Many other tractors of all sizes passed that year, including Ford's little four-cylinder. At less than half the weight of the Waterloo Boy N, the Fordson still pulled more than a ton on its drawbar; it achieved certification in June 1920 with Nebraska Test No. 18.

Just when Deere executives had something to celebrate, Henry Ford dropped his marketing bomb. In January 1921, he began cutting his basic Fordson tractor's price from $785 to $620, then to $395. International Harvester and Deere followed suit by slashing prices, though the rock-bottom Fordson still halved its competitors' price tags. Deere & Company's lowest possible price was $890.

Everyone, except the farmer, paid dearly for the discount rivalry. Ford lost more than 45 percent of sales in one year, down to 35,000 units. Deere sold fewer than 80 of the nearly

simply cannot provide for a greater nation while they are still reeling from economic uncertainty and tied to traditionalism.

Tractor sales mirrored farmers' hesitation toward turning to machine to boost their crop production. In 1919, U.S. farmers owned around 150,000 tractors but nearly 26.5 million horses and mules. And the farmers were skeptical about tractors for good reason. Affordability and quality rarely went hand in hand—not because technology lagged, but because industry standards were nonexistent. Of the 180

ONE DEERE BECOMES DEAR TO MANY

At age 32, John Deere had little choice but to leave his Vermont home for a chance to build a future out West. So he kissed his wife and first four children goodbye and made his way to Grand Detour, Illinois, in the winter of 1836. There he started up a successful blacksmithing business that would one day become the fourth oldest company in America. At the time, he couldn't possibly have known how people more than a century and a half later would cherish memorabilia from his company's journey.

A LEGEND GETS ESTABLISHED

By 1848, John Deere had moved his company 75 miles southwest of Grand Detour, to Moline, Illinois, where he had advantages of the water power and transportation routes provided by the Mississippi River. Deere and his wife Damarius had raised nine

children, the fifth of which, Charles, would become the company's next president. The business-minded Charles took over in 1859, when he was only 21 years old. Less than 10 years later, Deere's business, which had always been a partnership or single proprietorship company, was incorporated into Deere & Company, with John and Charles holding 65 percent of the shares.

But it's not only the success story that makes all things Deere a collector's dream. After mounting debts and a slump in new business caused financial struggle, Deere & Company cut its workers wages' by 10 percent. The decision led to a short-term strike by employees during the nation's centennial year. Sometime after the men came back to their jobs, a new symbol appeared as the company's trademark—a bounding deer.

Miscellaneous is the only word that truly describes the array of Deere & Company-related baubles, gizmos, and trinkets prized by today's collectors. This assortment includes a bottle of unlicensed Leaping Lager beer dreamt up by advertising agency account team, the 28th edition of "The Operation Care and Repair of Farm Machinery" booklet, a child's 1950s-circa straw hat, a 150th anniversary anvil paperweight, John Deere's walking plow in a 10-inch replica, a dual salt and pepper shaker (worth up to $100), Velie letter opener, several pins and buttons, an engine oil can charm, a spinning manure spreader pocket watch fob, a pearlized ballpoint pen, and a bullet lighter from the first John Deere Tractor Company in Waterloo, Iowa. *Nick Cedar*

THE ICON GROWS BY LEAPS AND BOUNDS

The deer jumping gracefully over a log might have alluded to John Deere's natural talent for manufacturing products that anticipated farmers' needs, or it even could have been an emblem of the company's ability to surmount the hurdles it faced during the first 40 years. Whatever the initial intent, though, the leaping deer became an illustrious mark of the quality in every Deere & Company product. As the founder of the company openly promised, "I will never put my name on an implement that hasn't in it the best that's in me."

And so through the many decades since the first logo, Deere & Company created countless items prominently displaying the trademark and John Deere name for its customers, employees, and the public.

Many of the trinkets and treasures were originally intended to support business or community relationships. Keepsakes range in glamour from one employee's engraved gold pocket watch, marking 50 years service upon retirement, to a myriad of thermometers or other gizmos used as giveaways by dealers. Items overlooked by many people in the past are today considered rare finds by Deere collectors. For example a 65-year-old pack of commonplace matches, never struck, that displays the Deere & Company logo with a two-cylinder tractor is valued up to $50. And promotional anniversary calendars from the same time frame are worth as much as $800.

Deere & Company's logo underwent seven redesigns throughout the twentieth century, all the while prominently positioning the JOHN DEERE moniker. The trademark has been honed from the artistic rendering of a full-bodied, long-antlered deer crossing a log to a profile silhouette of an eight-pointer mid-rise, "leaping forward" into the future of agriculture.

Many people have sought out or simply saved John Deere collectibles as tangible memoirs of bygone days. Others seek out the historical value that may reconnect them with the past, and still others hope to cash in on their green-and-gold goodies. Whatever the individual's motivation is for buying, savoring, or selling a piece of Deere & Company's history, it's apparent that John Deere's artisan talent, pioneering spirit, and never-faltering work ethic still draw collectors from around the world to "bleed green."

Quite popular among collectors, these gold-plated belt buckles are a fairly new trademarked item offered by Deere throughout the 1980s and early 1990s. Most belt buckles, which are reminiscent of Deere & Company product events and historical pinpoints, are worth less than $50, with the notable exception of the official employee uniform belt buckles issued from the 1940s and 1950s (not pictured). The coveted black and silver accessory picturing a four-legged deer, with its antlers upright, can fetch up to $600. *Nick Cedar*

Producing a series of gold-plated calendar medallions has been a Deere tradition for more than 20 years now. The medallions feature year-at-a-glance dates on the back and various symbols of company progress embossed on the face. The medallion pictured here is the millennium tribute to twentieth century logos in 2000. The most prized in any collection today would be, of course, the 1987 150th anniversary coin. *Nick Cedar*

800 tractors it built in 1921. Lack of demand for its Waterloo Boys forced Deere to produce only a few more than 300 tractors in 1922. Despite its pioneering success in the Nebraska Tests, Deere's somewhat outdated Waterloo Boy Model N couldn't compete effectively with the small, lightweight, much less expensive Fordson. To make matters worse, the 1923 spring crop disappointed farmers, who further tightened their belts around farm equipment purchases.

There was no corporate money or time to reinvent the Waterloo Boy tractor, but Deere had to make a change to improve sales. With unsold Waterloo Boy Ns left over, the company had the prebuilt engine power to add to its smaller and lighter model design. So they began experimenting to create the N's in-house successor. Only handfuls of each of

first three versions of Deere's new tractor, models A through C, made it out of production. The fourth, Model D, was the frontrunner for Deere's launch of its own tractor.

D-DAY

Deere & Company kept the price of its Model D at $1,000 and ordered 1,000 new tractors into production during mid-1923. Company executives intended to come to market with a better-made product than the Fordson, to gain a niche and to convince farmers that it was worth spending more on a Deere.

The D was a heavier-duty machine than Ford's Fordson but lighter and smaller than the Deere Waterloo Boy lines. The change in size and external appearance from the old Waterloo Boys made the Model D popular among farmers

continued on page 43

Much to the delight of farmers everywhere in 1926, the Model D was fitted with a solid flywheel keyed to the crankshaft. Operators everywhere moved more freely around their tractors. Another "solid" change: the end of slotted spokes in the steering wheel, which had dwindled from four holes in 1923 to three in 1924, then to two in 1925 before disappearing altogether on 1926 models.

With no frame and only two forward speeds, the early Model D plowed steadily along in sales on its 46-inch steel wheels and straight front axle.

These product literature pieces, from 1930 and 1935 respectively, promoted the latest in Model D innovations. As old as they might look now, these brochures had something new and exciting to tell farmers. The yellow-themed closed-cover brochure depicts a midline Model D that's already been made more safe by its solid flywheel. The more colorful spread in the open brochure shows how the Model D continued to evolve through the 1930s, with its exhaust and air intake prominently posted atop the hood. This more mature Model D had an increased engine size and produced a great deal more horsepower than the earlier models. The 1935 Model D finally gained a third forward gear, catching up to an industry standard set more than a decade earlier. *Nick Cedar*

NEBRASKA TEST No. 102 (1924)	
Tractor model	D (early)
Production years	1923–1927
Serial numbers	30401–53387
Drawbar rating (hp)	15
Belt pulley/PTO rating (hp)	27
Fuel	kerosene (run)/gasoline (start)

Known affectionately by farmers as the "Spoker," early Model Ds used large, spaciously six-spoked flywheels. Later considered too dangerous because it chewed up anything that slipped into it, the open-spoked flywheel was redesigned several times during the D's 30-year run. Eventually the D's reputation as a Bid Daddy tractor was strengthened not just by the improved safety of its more compact, enclosed flywheel, but because of the fortification of its cast axle and its mammoth pulling power of nearly two and a quarter tons.

Away from the field, steel extension rims protect the lugs on this Model D, as well as the pavement beneath, when its owner needs to take a little 3.25-mile-per-hour road trip.

Midway through 1927, beginning with serial number 53388, Deere engineers increased the bore on the Model D engine by .25 inches and splined the driveshaft to hold the flywheel.

Henry Dreyfuss tackled a new driver's seat design in 1937. Frustrated that he couldn't match his true-to-life human forms of various "Joe" and "Josephine" sizes to the seat, he asked where the original shape came from. Promptly, Dreyfuss was told it came from Pete, the guy in the shop with the biggest behind, who had sat in plaster to make the mold.

The Model D was the only early Deere-made tractor to use the engine and transmission housing as its frame.

The nickel-hole Model D tractors had safer "solid" flywheels, with one coin-sized opening in the center to accommodate the expansion and constriction of the iron cast. The nickel-hole design was short-lived, however. In standard operating conditions with fluctuating temperatures in the field, plenty of the 2,000 original "solid" flywheels eventually cracked. Later 1920s Model D flywheel designs used stress slots, which were capped at each end by larger diameter openings.

NEBRASKA TEST Nos. 146 (1926)/236 (1935)/350 (1940)

Tractor model	D (late)
Production years	1927–1953
Serial numbers	53388–191670
Drawbar ratings (hp)	15/24.02/30.46
Belt pulley/PTO ratings (hp)	27/37.37/38.11
Fuel	distillate (run)/gasoline (start)

Opposite and above

Identifiable from above as an earlier Model D by the absence of an exhaust stack and lack of styling, this mid-line tractor has several safety and power improvements over the Deere's initial versions. By waiting until 1928 to purchase a D, farmers got a machine with a slightly larger engine (going from a 6.5- to a 6.75-inch cylinder bore). The change added about 6 horsepower to both the drawbar and belt.

Above

Still sporting the 1937 John Deere logo, this 1948 styled Model D had an electric starter, an enclosed steering column, and an instrument panel that gave the driver a clearer understanding of how efficiently the tractor was running.

Opposite

Model Ds built after 1939 had the "Dreyfuss style" in mind and looked formidable with the vertical lines of their steely faces.

continued from page 34

from the start. And although sales started slowly, Deere turned the corner on its tractor division profits by 1925. Even as some farmers did well, many farmers never recovered from the war, and 7,872 of them went bankrupt that year—more than during any other year in the country's history.

Early on, the irregular pitch from the engine's two cylinders firing at the 180- and 560-degree rotation points of the crankshaft earned the Deere tractors farmer-forged nicknames.

For many years to come, they would be known as Johnny Poppers, poppin' Johnnys, two-lungers, or two-bangers.

Despite the nicknames, the love affair between farmers and their yellow-and-green tractors didn't blossom overnight. The already frail economy of the 1920s meant less room for error by Deere leaders in formulating the company's long-term tractor marketing strategy. Farmers wouldn't settle for just any tractor. Improving the solid design of the Model D

would likely muster sales margins that sheer volume production couldn't. The company decided a little remodeling was the place to start.

Because the first 50 Model Ds essentially used that same engine as the Waterloo Boy Model N, Deere & Company was eager to increase ownership in its tractor design. Changes to the first Deere-born tractor began nearly instantaneously with production of the 51st Model D and would continue throughout the tractor's 30-year production run. First, the company changed the welding front into a casting, which strengthened the axle.

When the spoked version, called the Spoker, became a limb-mangling danger to farmers, the company introduced the nearly solid "nickel-hole" flywheel. In 1927, the tractor had a bigger engine; the cylinder bore was increased from 6.5 inches to 6.75. By the early 1930s, the tractor had gained 500 pounds, its steering had gone from the right side to the left and back to the right, and engine speed had increased to 900 rpm.

In 1935, the Model D's newly added third forward gear trailed the industry's four-speed transmission trend, but it moved the company forward another step. In their effort to get up to speed with the competition, Deere executives realized the room for improvement on the Model D was more than a simple tractor redesign would allow. It was time to build something new.

But for a tractor to be created from the ground up, Deere would have to rest on the laurels of the current D for maybe two model years. A move like that would allot more time to the competition, such as International Harvester, which already offered thousands of farmers an irresistible row-crop tractor with a catchy name and pick-pocket price tag—the $825 Farmall.

The late-styled Model D was a mature tractor, qualified by years of design improvements that included an electric start, a vertical exhaust and air intake, a power takeoff, rubber tires, a three-speed transmission, and rear wheel brakes.

Chapter 3

A NEW FACE IN TRACTORS

Cs, GPs, and Crawlers Are Experimental and Special

As the Roaring Twenties came to an end, farmers were looking for more in their tractors than just reliable pulling machines—they wanted versatility. They wanted something that could help with multiple tasks, something that was capable of tilling, planting, harvesting, and weeding fragile crops. They wanted something that performed in any situation like a trusty old horse.

International Harvester first brought a truly versatile tractor into the marketplace in 1924, the year after Deere's D launch, with its immediately popular Farmall tractor. Conceptually, the small, all-purpose tractor's design was innovative

Previous pages
Produced four years after the last Waterloo Boy Model N, this 1928 Model C wears the John Deere logo and green-and-yellow paint without any presence of red. The C is a link to the modern tractor, with a forward-facing radiator merging with the sheet metal that shelters the engine and contains the fuel tank.

from front to back. The Farmall's four-wheel tricycle configuration—in which the two front wheels were close together—its high-clearance frame, sleek body, and multiple rear and forward implement attachment points combined to make the four-cylinder machine a material marvel. Such a design could handle the finesse jobs of weeding delicate crops that a bulky tractor couldn't, making it useful throughout the growing season. But Harvester didn't flood the country with its masterpiece. Instead, the first 200 hand-built Farmalls showed up only in areas where the company's sales were lagging, and dealers concentrated their efforts more on the proven McCormick-Deering 10-20 and 15-30 models.

From the get-go, Deere knew it had to match tractor ingenuity with an all-purpose design. But starting from scratch would take more years out of the marketplace than the company could afford. John Deere's great-grandson, Charles Deere Wiman, a former line employee in the shop, made his biggest impact as director of manufacturing in 1925 when he directed the John Deere Plow Works Experimental Department to build a not-so-new, all-purpose tractor.

The Model C offered farmers four power sources: its drawbar, a PTO, a mechanical power lift, and a belt pulley. With its bowed front axle and automotive-type steering, the Model C had good clearance. Note the deep lugs on the rear wheels that were useful for work in the fields.

Like its predecessors, the Model C two-cylinder started on gasoline and ran on kerosene. Although not tested at Nebraska, the C used the same L-head engine as the GP, which scored 17.24 drawbar and just under 25 belt horsepower. The tractor was not up to farmers' demands, though, and frequent breakdowns and the unorthodox three-row cultivator configuration gave it a short life.

LET'S 'C' WHAT WE CAN DO

It didn't take long to get the basic design in order. Deere's answer to "all-purpose" was the Model C tractor. In the interest of saving Deere and Company's time and money, the Model C was purposefully similar to a Model D in engine design and a certain overall look, but the C offered some breakthrough and controversial features. The high-arched front axle added to the basic D front-end design molded the C into a three-row cultivator, immediately singling it out from two- and four-row competition. Rightfully, Deere & Company board members wondered what benefit could come from such an irregular characteristic. Conversely, the tractor offered the irrefutable benefits of power lift for implements, individual rear brakes, and a 520-rpm power takeoff (PTO). Limited to 10 horsepower by its engine size, however, the $800 Model C wouldn't be as attractive a proposition as the $600 Farmall.

As if price and performance weren't enough to consider, the model's alphabetical succession also caused concern among board members. The phonetics of the letter C might easily be confused with the letter D during orders taken over temperamental rural phone lines. The tractor needed a different name. Consistent with Deere's goals for recognition of both its brand and its versatility, the Model C became the Model GP, for "General Purpose."

With Farmalls already selling in the thousands each year, Wiman couldn't wait for the newly named GP to become something it was not without an extensive redesign. So in early 1928, after building only a hundred or so Model Cs, Deere's soon-to-be fourth-generation leader gave the go-ahead on the $3.9 million tooling-up process for the GP's first production run at the Waterloo factory.

This 1928 GPWT (wide tread) demonstrates the classic tricycle design. The front wheels pass between two crop rows, while the latter wheels straddle both rows.

NEBRASKA TEST No. 153 (1928)	
Tractor model	C and GP (early)
Production years	1927–1930
Serial numbers	200211–223802
Drawbar rating (hp)	10
Belt pulley/PTO rating (hp)	20
Fuel	kerosene (run)/gasoline (start)

The early C and GP group includes the first model GPWT, number 40000 (400000–405254), built August 20, 1929, and shipped to Tynan, Texas. This series also marks the beginning of specialty crop models, with number P5000, a "Potato Special," built January 30, 1930, and shipped to Mattituck, New York.

As the pictures suggest, the GPWT shares its engine, transmission, and general appearance with the Model C. The main difference between this GP wide tread and the C is the axle configuration, though some mechanical changes were made to address failings that surfaced on the C.

TINKER TILL IT'S RIGHT

The GP, rated as a two-plow tractor, didn't grab Deere a spot in the all-purpose market at first. A myriad of problems plagued the GP's introduction. Engineers had hastily built some of the original GPs simply to maximize the horsepower in a Deere-named tractor. Where farmers pushed the machines, they were breaking down—many needing to be rebuilt in the fields. Meanwhile, southern cotton growers weren't adapting to the three-row cultivation scheme, and no matter what the crop, operators still had a hulk of a tractor to partially obstruct their view on all sides.

True tractor failures were sure to mean industry losses. Even the affordable little Fordson couldn't ride on its low price forever. Plagued with product shortcomings, Ford left tractor manufacturing in 1928. Fortunately, the Model D continued to carry Deere's sales, keeping the company in the number two position, now behind International Harvester.

It was time for Deere to tackle the GP problems head on, abandoning consistency in styling in favor of staying in business. Redesign, from the ground up, was necessary to produce a true competitor to the Farmall.

Wiman's experimental department went on to create a Deere GP tricycle in 1928, with two close front wheels and a 50-inch rear tread. A handful of these models had a special 68-inch tread to cover two potato rows, a design that would lead to a potato-specific GP series. But farmers below the Corn Belt continued to reject the three-row concept in favor of the popular two- and four-row cultivation standard. Deere wouldn't settle for a partial market, and the last of only 72 GP tricycles ever built was shipped to Maine on April 19, 1929.

Deere saw that its market would reach farther with longer axles. The first GPWT, WT standing for wide tread, built in

Proper lubrication was essential to the tractor's functioning capability and longevity. Since many farmers were still new to mechanized farming, Deere placed the lubrication instructions on the GP right in front of the steering wheel on the back end of the gas tank.

1929, was shipped to Tynan, Texas. With its new 76-inch rear tread, which straddled two typical crop rows, the line of GPWTs was a hot seller from North to South. In its initial run from 1929 to 1930, more than 2,000 GPWTs rolled off the assembly line with 5.75x6-inch (bore and stroke) engines.

NEBRASKA TEST No. 190 (1931)	
Tractor model	GP (late)
Production years	1930–1935
Serial numbers	223803–230745
Drawbar rating (hp)	15.52
Belt pulley/PTO rating (hp)	24.30
Fuel	distillate (run)/gasoline (start)

Includes GPWT and GPO (14994–15732) orchard models with deep-skirted fenders. The Lindemans of Yakima, Washington, built the first GPO by retrofitting an existing GP in 1929; later they added crawler tracks. The first serial number GPO with molded hard rubber tires, 15257, was built May 31, 1932, and was shipped to Palatka, Florida. The first low-pressure balloon tire GPO model came 18 months later.

The plow of choice for the two-plow rated GP was this Model 4B. The combination is easy enough to operate that even this young farmer can get the job done.

Solid front wheels and wide rear fenders were additional design touches to the GPO Experimental and were intended to keep branches from getting caught on the tractor, which was primarily used in orchard farming.

Similar to the GPWT were a group of GP tractors with wider-than-standard rear treads made for fields growing the Northeast's specialty crop—potatoes. They were called Series P tractors. Riding on a 68-inch tread width and special wheels, a group of about 200 GPP tractors were sold to potato growers in the Northeast over eight months in 1930. But the stock market crash of 1929 had wreaked havoc on the agricultural economy, and Deere had to keep its production efficiency high in its 1930s operations. So the company discontinued the specialty P in favor of one GPWT that still accommodated potato growers' needs. This GPWT modification used convertible dished wheels to obtain the necessary tread width on a standardized axle. The factory also continued making the potato "bedding" parallel front wheels as an option.

It started life with a 5.75x6-inch engine, but the Model GP eventually matured into a 6x6-inch L-head bore and stroke that rated 95 rpm in models from 1930–1935. Its later engine gave the two-and-a-half-ton tractor nearly 15 percent more pulling power, getting the horsepower up to 15.52 on the drawbar and 24.30 power takeoff at the belt.

One of the advantages of mechanized farming is mechanized planting. Farmers who bought the Model 301 three-row planter for their GP tractor reported satisfactory service, but the market didn't buy into the three-row approach.

With its relatively modern profile and rubber tires, this GP would fool a lot of onlookers into thinking it was made a lot later than 1929.

Deere continued upgrading the features of its General Purpose tractors throughout the early 1930s. In 1932, the company introduced yet another new GPWT with several improvements. The hood was tapered for increased ground visibility, steering was made easier by moving the front wheel axles onto a spindle mount, spark and throttle controls were relocated onto the steering support for more fluent acceleration, and adjustable cushion springs supported the driver's seat for the first time.

ECONOMY, NOT INNOVATION, HIT BY DEPRESSION

During the same years in which Deere was improving its general-purpose tractor line, the number of on-farm tractors reached the one million mark in the United States. Although farmers seemed to be adopting tractors in monumental numbers, the 1930 census reported that still less than 15 percent of farmers reported owning a tractor.

Those who did own tractors cut their labor hours in half per bushel of corn and by more than 60 percent per bushel of wheat, when compared with those farmers using turn-of-the-century-farming practices. But higher productivity served only to further afflict the farm economy, and land values plummeted at the onset of the Great Depression. Once averaging $69 per acre in 1920, farmland values dropped 37 percent in just three years, to $30 in 1933, and land stayed below $33 an acre for the rest of the 1930s.

Only 38 tractor makers remained in 1930 and by 1933, tough times hit Deere & Company, as only 765 of its tractors sold that year. But the continuity of its two-cylinder D, GP, and GPWT models helped the manufacturer survive the early years of the Great Depression. The company's Midwest-based engineers also had more innovations in the works and were getting outside input from more than 1,000 miles away that would lead to additional variations on established equipment—not to mention some newfangled machines that were still on the Deere drawing board.

NEW MARKETS GROW ON TREES

Deere engineers developed new versions of their tractors based on emerging markets nationwide. One such adaptation of Deere's all-purpose success cropped up in Yakima, Washington.

Greatly dependent on weather and changing markets, the apple industry's output and prices fluctuated from year to year. In 1930, more than 156 million bushels of apples were produced, selling for $1.02 per bushel. This reflected a price trend that had declined somewhat since 1917 but generally continued in the low $1 range. After 1931, when a crop of more than 200 million bushels fetched farmers only $.66 per bushel, apples would reach $1.00 again only once in the whole decade.

Mechanized power was an important investment to increase the apple growers' efficiency with such indecisive market returns, but the looser sand-based soils and uneven slopes of the Pacific Northwest's orchards required the might and grip of crawler tracks on orchard tractors.

The GP was one of the first two-cylinder tractors to utilize an oil-bath air cleaner.

The Lindeman Company converted two dozen Model GP tractors to crawler drive so that they could maneuver easily through apple orchards in the Northwest. This is a 1935 Model GPO Lindeman crawler.

Like the C, the GP wore the Deere logo down the side of the gas tank, as well as across the top of the radiator. The air cleaner on this 1930 GPO Experimental is laid back and runs along the motor to a spot behind the wide fenders, out of reach of low-hanging branches. The exhaust pipe was moved from the left to right side of these tractors, giving them the nickname "Crossover."

The solution to the problem would come from a 30-year-old named Jesse Lindeman. He had already been in the tractor business in Washington State for a few years, building a solid reputation as a crawler dealer, when his franchise, a Cletrac dealership, started faltering. The head of Cletrac had fiddled with his company's product line to the point that the quality of the product started declining. So in 1930, Lindeman turned his family business into a John Deere full-line dealership, based on the proven power and performance of the Model D.

The tree-fruit farmers who were Lindeman's customers liked the D's economical fuel system, but they had no use for its wheels. Lindeman came up with a plan—he engineered a handmade crawler D, retrofitted with a set of Best Model 30 tracks and rollers left over in his shop.

Steering was more than a bit of an issue on the machine, however. Using track brakes without clutches to direct the tractors was the only type of control system Lindeman had for his crawlers. Even with the steering problem, Lindeman's modification attracted attention. One of Jesse's younger brothers tested the machine in the region where it caught the eyes of other farmers, for whom Lindeman built two more. Soon the Lindeman family was one-upping the manufacturer with the dealership's modest sales accomplishment as farmers chose Lindeman's crawlers to fertilize, weed, and haul carts of apples in their orchards. Because Deere & Company realized that the Lindemans were continuing to order tractors without wheels to make their own crawlers, its representatives paid Jesse and his brothers a visit. Quietly, Deere commissioned Lindeman to draw up an official design that turned the standard GP into a GPO for "General Purpose Orchard" work.

Lindeman's new GPO came with elongated fender options to protect low-hanging produce. He also lowered the tractor's height and added his trademark crawler tracks. But getting the steering right was more of a challenge, due to the limits of the brake-controlled system. The outside track spun faster than the halted inside track on turns, which made the machine speed up in a curve. Still, the tractor did the job, and Lindeman's 24 John Deere GPOs, eventually titled John Deere Lindemans, crawled into history by 1935.

Deere began developing its own crawler Model Ds in July 1930 but quit less than a month later because its wheel brakes couldn't satisfactorily control the prototypes. Eventually, most of the Lindeman-contrived GPO crawlers were refitted with a better steering system that used clutches to disengage the drive from the inner track, thereby giving the farmer a slower, more controlled feel in the turns. Lindeman's design led to a permanent market for future Deere crawler models, such as the BO Lindeman crawler tractor, which sold nearly 1,700 units through the mid-1940s.

Above

Lindeman's earliest crawler, built from a Model D with tracks from a Best crawler, was a handful. It steered by braking one side, which caused the differential to send power to the other track. By the time the GPO shown here was produced, Lindeman and his engineers had figured out steering clutches. All but one of the GPO Lindeman's were fitted or retrofitted with them.

Opposite

This Lindeman GPO is outfitted with rubber tracks to avoid damaging asphalt or concrete surfaces.

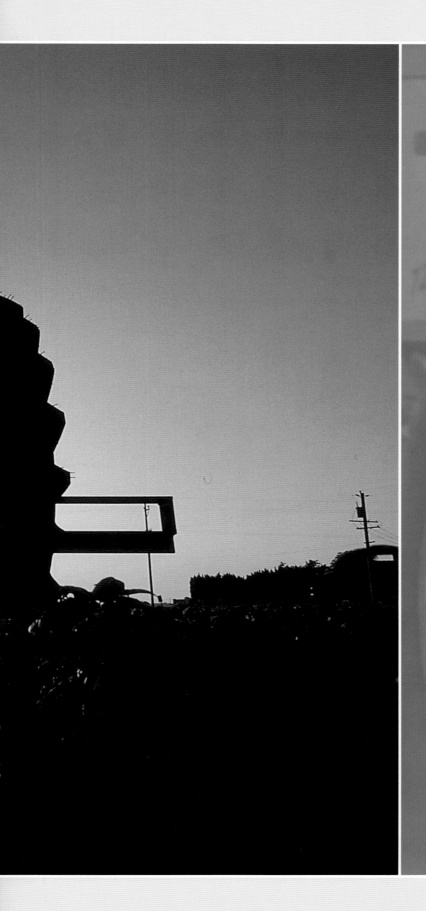

Chapter 4

A BEFORE B, EVEN AFTER C

Deere's Power and Versatility Pick Up Speed

By the early 1930s, most manufacturers had refined the working mechanics of their tractors. The next big innovation in the tractor world came with the perfection of low-pressure pneumatic rubber tires, which first became an option in 1932. Though not fit for every field, tires meant a much smoother ride than was possible with the steel wheels used previously. The rubber tires also provided greater traction in many field situations.

Despite being skeptical that traction would slip with tires, farmers were soon impressed by the fuel efficiency rubber tire–fitted tractors provided. They also

Deere & Company advertised the Model BN as the "Garden Tractor" for farmers. The little production tractor originally came on steel wheels. But the single-front wheeled BN proved more useful to many farmers with rubber tires, so Deere just cut down the steel and welded on new rims to accommodate the tires.

noticed that they became less fatigued when riding on these tractors. For these reasons, they adopted the rubber tire quickly. In fact, the response to rubber tire–equipped tractors was so overwhelming that the National Bureau of Economic Research later documented the phenomenon. In 1935, 14 percent of all tractors were made with rubber tires, but by 1940 more than 90 percent of all tractors were driven off the assembly line on tires.

With such a demand, rubber tires became a natural fit for Deere's new alphabetical series lineup of all-purpose trac-

tors. Models B and A became the follow-ups to Deere's C model. Using traditional two-cylinder I-head engines in both models, Deere created many versions of each series to meet nearly every specialized farm duty.

Because of its greater mass and more massive capabilities, the four-speed, 4,000-pound Model A debuted first, in early 1934. The new tractors solved two big dilemmas for farmers: the need for something other than fixed treads, which had forced farmers to plant rows according to the width of their tractors' wheels, and eliminating offset hitch points, which caused implements to trail at strange angles behind the tractor.

Designers made the initial Model A two plow–rated tractor more versatile than any Deere to date. The adjustable rear-track width let farmers decide from 56 to 84 inches how wide their rows would be. Engineers enclosed the transmission housing, which increased ground clearance over the previous two-piece casting, and successfully moved the power takeoff and hitch to work from the center of the tractor. By eliminating

A 1938 Model AW burned kerosene or distillate fuel, the convenience of which would soon be referred to by Deere in its promotional literature as "All-Fuel" compatibility. Later on that year, the adjustable-front unstyled AW was given a Henry Dreyfuss facelift and upgraded to a four-speed transmission.

ompared to a Big A row-cropper, the toy-sized control area of early Model Bs could make the driver feel like a kid again. Though its physical presence was small, the 9 horsepower Model B proved big with farmers because of its versatility and 16 variations, well-suited for nearly every type of operation.

angled implements and resultant side-draft effects, the Model A four-wheel tricycle gave farmers greater confidence in the accuracy of their pulling.

The Model A was a strong and economical addition to the Deere family, with its 6.5x7-inch engine rating 16.22 horsepower at the drawbar and 23.52 from the belt in its original Nebraska Test, No. 222. Once it was fired up on gasoline, the engine could run on either kerosene or other inexpensive distillate fuels. The A also offered a converted power-lift system that gave farmers their first-ever boost of hydraulic power. The hydraulics eased equipment movement, cushioning the drop of implements so that farmers could have more control in their fieldwork.

continued on page 68

This very first production Model B must have grown up in some serious muck. Serial number 1000 is a general purpose tricycle with dished wheels in front and skeleton wheels in back to navigate through heavy, wet soils. It was built on October 2, 1934, and originally shipped to Dallas. It is one of a small minority of unstyled Model Bs fitted with a four-bolt pedestal attachment.

NEBRASKA TEST Nos. 222 (1934)/335 (1939)

Tractor model	A (early)
Production years	1934–1940
Serial numbers	410008–498999
Drawbar rating (hp)	16.22/20.12
Belt pulley/PTO rating (hp)	23.52/26.33
Fuel	distillate (run)/gasoline (start)

Includes styled and unstyled models, 14 variations in all of the AI, A-GP (later just Model A), AN, ANH, AR, AW, AWH, AO, and AOS.

NEBRASKA TEST No. 232

Tractor model	B (early)
Production years	1935–1938
Serial numbers	1000–59999
Drawbar rating (hp)	9.28
Belt pulley/PTO rating (hp)	14.25
Fuel	distillate (run)/gasoline (start)

Includes 16 different models (styled and unstyled): B-GP (or B), BI, BN, BNH, BO, BR, BW, BW-40 (shorter frame), BWH, and BWH-40. A crawler orchard version created by the Lindemans, called the BO Lindeman, was not considered as one of Deere & Company's product lineup but was recognized by farmers and dealers as a valid Deere tractor.

NEBRASKA TEST Nos. 305 (1938)/366 (1941)

Tractor model	B (mid)
Production years	1938–1947
Serial numbers	60000–200999
Drawbar rating (hp)	10.76/14.08
Belt pulley/PTO rating (hp)	16.86/17.46
Fuel	distillate (run)/gasoline (start)

Opposite

Early Model Bs, built before 1937, had shorter frames, at 44.5 inches, and hood lengths, at 42.5 inches, than their successors. This 1936 Model B had a 4.25x5.25-inch All-Fuel engine.

A AND B—FIT FOR EVERY FARM

Throughout the 1930s and 1940s, Deere & Company stuck to its strategy of reaching every type, size, and shape of farm with its various tractor types, sizes, and shapes. By using this sales approach, which gave farmers the options they were looking for, Deere had production variations of many different model lines, most of which came in its long-lived A and B model lines. Because of the popularity of these lines, along with the several variations, they accounted for more than half a million sales by the 1950s.

Although the name variations were straightforward in the A and B lines, usually implying the exact configuration of the tractor's axle, wheels, and tread—N for narrow, NH for narrow-high, O for orchard, R for regular, W for wide, and WH for wide-high—the names alone didn't explain just how Deere's two biggest-selling two cylinder models were adapted to meet every farmer's needs.

When the Model A made its debut in 1934, American agriculture was barely surviving the economic devastation caused by the Great Depression. Farmers weren't fairing well, and neither was the tractor industry—only 30 or so companies were still in business, down from the 186 tractor makers that were operating less than a decade before. But the century-old Deere & Company had experienced times like these before, and it was only a matter of time until the country would make a turnaround.

The executives decided the best way to outlive the economic downtrend, and maybe even change the cycle for agriculture, was through superior mechanical innovation and farmer satisfaction. The company was poised to bring its solution to market.

THE ALPHA—MODEL A

Deere & Company advertised its Model A as a "greatly improved" and "more powerful tractor," one that could get even the largest row-crop farmer's work done "at lowest cost" and "on-time, ahead of bad weather, and when field and crop conditions are right."

A farmer could change the rear tread setting on his tricycle ANH to straddle his variable row spacing by simply adjusting the rims. The back wheels were 40 inches in diameter, instead of 36 inches. The mandatory pneumatic rubber tires on the high-crop variations added a good deal more clearance under the axle.

The name fits this tractor. It's literally A Wide-High, with wide, adjustable front-end extensions that encompassed double rows. Serial numbers 469668–476999 encompass all the unstyled, high-clearance Model As through 1938.

The new tractor had several big redesigns that got farmers' attention. One of the most instantly recognizable was the adoption of pneumatic rubber tires, which were similar in design to tires used on aircraft. Another was the one-piece transmission housing that created higher clearance under the axle and centered the drawbar and PTO shaft for more accurate, efficient pulling of field implements.

Deere & Company caught up to the industry with the Model A by adding individual left and right brakes that directed the large drive gears with greater ease to the operator and gave more longevity to the machine. And with the flip of a switch, farmers now had smoother implement placement and control with a self-contained hydraulic system that replaced the lever-activated mechanical lift system of the GP.

But the tractor industry had never experienced adjustable wheel tread before. With a span of 56 to 80 inches in the Model A's sliding rear axle, this tractor offered farmers the most flexibility available in row-crop farming for the day.

The different models of the A series began cropping up immediately following the general purpose tractor's unveiling. The following four row-crop versions came out as a result: the AN, a narrower single front-wheel tricycle model; the AW, with an adjustable, widefront axle; the ANH, a narrow tricycle with the front wheel enlarged by 6 inches; and the AWH, a widefront, high-clearance model. Both H-designated models came factory-standard with only pneumatic tires, the greater clearance made possible by 40-inch rear wheels instead of 36-inch wheels.

This rear view is a rare peek at the BWH-40, as true John Deere two-cylinder enthusiasts know. Only a dozen of these little tractors were produced with narrow-tired wide fronts, which were adjustable from 40.62 inches all the way up to 80.62 inches, depending on whether the farmer used 7- and 13-inch extensions. Also, the rear wheels were removable and reversible, making for two sets of tread differentials. The wheels varied up to 13.5 inches on the inside setting, or 21.25 inches with the rims adjusted outward.

But the A wasn't just for row crops. The AR, or Model A Regular, offered standard, fixed tread to grain and grass farmers. The AR was lower to the ground and stouter than the row-crop A versions. Also, the AR had a single brake and no hydraulic

This narrow highboy Model B obviously received the Henry Dreyfuss treatment. Although it retained a regular "Pete-sized" seat, at least the electric starter was an option this year.

lift. Although it seemingly had none of the newly touted A-list features that farmers wanted, the Model AR still improved upon what farmers need most—power.

That power transferred nicely into an industrial version of the A. The AI donned different colors off the farm, but did the same heavy work as it had from 1936 to 1941.

The orchard spin-off of the AR was the AO, which had the addition of the row-crop A's differential brakes. First built in May 1936, the AO was replaced shortly after by the AOS, a "streamlined" version of the orchard tractor. Special features, such deep-skirted fenders and as an exhaust pipe redirected out the rear of the tractor, brought more overhead- and side-clearance for the tractor that often operated under low-hanging fruit trees. The AO design continued fairly unchanged until the introduction of the "New Improved AO," styled by Henry Dreyfuss and launched with six speeds and a bigger 5.5x6.75-inch engine.

Dreyfuss' styling of the Model A series gave most of the machines a new look in 1938. The Dreyfuss facelift was one of three over-hauls in the chronology of the Model A's 18-year lifespan, from the unstyled early models of 1934 through 1938 to the styled four-speeds (1938 to 1940), the styled models with six speeds and a .25-inch larger engine stroke (1941 through 1947), and finally, the late-styled AO and AR models from 1947 through 1953.

Dreyfuss also centered the exhaust and air intake pipes on the hood of all styled tractors so that operators could have a better view. The original muffler on all Model As was never taller than the intake pipe, but replacement mufflers were sometimes longer.

THE OMEGA—MODEL B

Introduced almost simultaneously with its larger sibling, the first Model B, serial number 1000, was built on Tuesday, October 2, 1934, just six months after the first Model A.

The two-thirds proportioned Model B had as much to offer as its big brother in the way of design standards, including four forward speeds and the farmer's choice of either solid steel wheels with 4-inch spade lugs, the more thickly spiked "skeleton wheels" for harder soils, or the comfortable pneumatic rubber tires in 7.5- or 9-inch width. The row-crop B also boasted all the advancements of adjustable wheel spacing, hydraulics, separate brakes, and had an economical price tag. But none of the standard-tread models—the lowboy Model BR, the industrial BI, or the orchard Model BO—offered adjustable rear tread, hydraulics, or left and right brakes, with the exception of the orchard model, which required the great control of differential braking.

Like the A, the Model B underwent many changes during its life. With the designations of general purpose B (or B-GP), BI, BN (or "Garden Tractor"), BNH, BO, BR, BW, or BWH, the smaller tractor gloriously sold more than any other John Deere two-cylinder model, including the Model A.

A small number of extremely specialized models, the BW-40 and BWH-40, were sold to California vegetable growers in San Francisco and Sacramento during the mid-1930s. Both of these models had adjustable front and back axles. The six BW-40s built in 1936 allowed growers to expand the front wheels between 40 to 52 inches and the rear wheels from 40 to 72 inches. The dozen BWH-40s produced not only had higher clearance, but also had wheels that maximized row spacing at more than 80 inches in front, using a 13-inch extension, and 80 inches in rear tread, with the rims set on the outer position.

The late-styled Bs, BNs, and BWs of 1947 to 1952 had solid pressed steel frames, a bigger bore in their engines at 4.69 inches, six-speed transmissions, interchangeable front-end assemblies, and a rear tread that straddled up to an amazing 84 inches.

The Model B rounded out Deere & Company's market reach, allowing the company to come full circle with its farmer-audience. Whether a farm had 1,000 acres or less than 100, Deere & Company at long last had built a general purpose tractor to fit every farm.

Farmers could see miles beyond their fields riding atop this specialty conversion of a styled Model B general purpose tractor, serial number 61338, which was retrofitted to this size somewhere in Montana. This very tall tractor has a 6-foot clearance underneath its rear axle, which is necessary to complete its purpose of spraying tassled corn.

Continued from page 61

Not to be outdone in sheer size, the official 1935 launch of the Model B, with its modest 4.25x5.25-inch All-Fuel engine, heralded the equal modernization of small farming equipment. At the original 9.28 horsepower drawbar and 14.25 belt horsepower rating, the B was physically a two-thirds version of its sizable counterpart. But the Model B had everything else the Model A did, including farmer demand.

Versatility was the key selling point for the constantly evolving As and Bs. The need for standard tread was prevalent in regions that grew grass crops, such as wheat and rice, so Deere came out with "regular" versions in 1935, models AR and BR, with fixed tread.

Almost immediately, specialty versions of the A and B continued to emerge. The narrow ANs and BNs had single front tires; the wide-front AWs and BWs sported adjustable front axles; an "H" extension was added on high-clearance narrow and wide models, which came only with pneumatic tires; and, of course, the orchard variants made tractors lower to the ground, with the air intake and exhaust stacks level to the hood. A limited number of narrow and wide and high-clearance Bs even had adjustable front axles, allowing vegetable growers to span their 20-inch rows. All versions and variations considered, including 14 Model As and 16 Bs, Deere

& Company produced approximately 600,000 of the two tractors—roughly 300,000 of each—in less than 20 years.

STYLE ISN'T FASHIONABLE, IT'S FUNDAMENTAL

When President Franklin D. Roosevelt took office in 1933, he brought with him a New Deal for the American people, including the farmers. In March 1933, less than two weeks after his inauguration and the famous four-day federal bank holiday that resulted in the Emergency Banking Act, Roosevelt addressed Congress with a strong message about agriculture:

"At the same time that you and I are joining in emergency action to bring order to our banks, and to make our regular Federal expenditure balance our income, I deem it of equal importance to take other and simultaneous steps without waiting for a later meeting of Congress. One of these is of definite, constructive importance to our economic recovery.

"It relates to agriculture and seeks to increase the purchasing power of our farmers and the consumption of articles manufactured in our industrial communities, and at the same time greatly to relieve the pressure of farm mortgages and to increase the asset value of farm loans made by our banking institutions. . . ." The speech was a prelude to Roosevelt's creation of several government agencies and

NEBRASKA TEST Nos. 378 (1941 Model AR)/384 (1947)/429 (1949 Model AR)

Tractor model	A (late)
Production years	1941–1952
Serial numbers	499000–703384
Drawbar rating (hp)	20.35/26.48/26.16
Belt pulley/PTO rating (hp)	26.30/33.53/33.24
Fuel	gasoline

NEBRASKA TEST Nos. 380 (1947)/381 (1947 All-Fuel)

Tractor model	B (late)
Production years	1947–1952
Serial numbers	201000–310775
Drawbar ratings (hp)	19.13/16.64
Belt pulley/PTO ratings (hp)	24.39/20.68
Fuel	gasoline/All-Fuel

INDUSTRIAL REVOLUTION ON WHEELS

No one had to strong-arm the agricultural clientele into buying Deere products in the early 1930s, as they clamored for more and more modified tractors. But Deere sales manager Frank Silloway was looking to sell Deere tractors to a new type of customer during the Great Depression.

Since 1926, Deere had been producing an "Industrial" version of its tractors. In the Model DI, "industrial" simply meant adding solid rubber tires, which were a standard characteristic of all Ds after 1927. But these industrial versions of the Model D never caught on. For the most part they were used within Deere & Company manufacturing to do heavy lifting around the John Deere Works. In fact, only a few DIs went to work beyond the company's foundries.

With pressurized tires now fast-becoming a standard feature for all types of vehicles, Silloway wanted to reach blue-collar businesses that needed tire-driven tractor power. In 1935, he found an industrial opportunity at the Caterpillar Tractor Company. By facilitating several Deere and Caterpillar meetings, Silloway helped form a deal between the manufacturers that gave Deere a new market for its industrial line of tractors. Caterpillar didn't want to diverge from its popular crawler models but needed to offer its dealerships a wheeled product to sell for certain applications. The outcome was a joint marketing arrangement, whereby Deere dealers could sell CAT machines and CAT dealers would show Deere "industrial" versions to the nonagricultural sector.

Of course, the sale of a John Deere tractor line that targeted an industry segment different from farming meant

This 1936 Industrial Model B was one of only 181 produced by Deere & Company during the five-year span that ended with the onset of World War II. At 115 inches long and 53.75 inches wide, the BI was the squattest of the line.

that the product had to be unique among Deere's lineup. Yet it still had to be recognizable as a Deere machine. So, with Deere Engineering Decision 6100, approving the first Model AI to be built to specifics, Industrial Yellow became a regular shade in Deere's color palette.

The first AI, serial number 252334, rolled off production lines on April 27, 1936, and was shipped to Columbus, Ohio. In 1937, the AI tractor sold for $1,395. The flush, orchard-style air intakes and horizontal exhaust systems improved both visibility and air quality for the driver. Similar modifications to other Deere farm tractors created new DIs and BIs, and a fully illustrated catalog advertised the entire industrial line.

The new yellow-and-black Deere market was barely off the starting line, producing less than a few hundred of all models, when the company shut down production of its industrial line on July 1, 1941, to prepare for World War II. For John Deere, the next three and a half years would be spent in filling limitation orders for civilian farm equipment production, as well as repair parts and exports. The company also devoted much of those years, and its assembly lines, to producing ammunition, airplane parts, laundry machines, and tank transmissions for the Allied forces.

Above

This Industrial yellow Deere Model A, serial number 252334, is the very first AI. It rolled off of the assembly line on April 27, 1936, headed for Columbus, Ohio, at a cost close to $1,400. Like all early As, the AI models used a 5.5x6.5-inch engine under the hood and an offset radiator cap on top.

Right

Although the early As were unstyled models, they soon offered operators several ergonomic comforts later employed in styled models. Padded, upholstered seats were standard in these AIs and were optionally made to swing toward either side for easier sight and maneuvering in reverse. Although AIs were based on the AR design, they also employed a few advantageous AO features, such as a side exhaust and flush-mounted air intake. The front windowpane opened upward in this tractor's tin and glass aftermarket cab.

This early unstyled Model A looks antiquated next to this late-styled Model A. In addition to the obvious wheel, grill, and cast-body design changes, the latter offered a noticeable seating improvement that farmers loved.

agriculture programs aimed at reducing crop surpluses and increasing farm income.

Over time, the New Deal helped farmers regain their operating capital and gave them room to breathe, which in turn meant room for them to spend a little on new equipment. By the latter part of the mid-1930s, farmers were looking once again to amass their fieldworker fleets.

Deere & Company, too, had turned the corner on the Depression. Rebounding from net tractor manufacturing losses in 1931 through 1933, the company hit $100 million in gross sales during 1937. But there still was room for improvement on its products. An industry leader in most regards, Deere lagged in an important feature of its tractor design—the polished look of a high-performance machine. Deere's tractors were

The difference that 10 years made in height and shape is obvious with these Model As. The older A has a more bulbous air intake design and taller reach on both its exhaust and air, which are situated side by side. In contrast, the styled A has vertically aligned pipes that are shorter and stockier.

The most noticeable change Henry Dreyfuss made on all Deere two-cylinder models from 1938 to 1959 was abandoning the overhead steering configuration in favor of sleeker design lines.

modern; engineers continuously improved their workmanship. The problem was that the green-and-yellow machines looked outdated, boxy, and utilitarian. Farmers yearned for their technology-driven purchases to look and feel as high-tech as the performance suggested.

Industrial design was in order, and vice president Elmer McCormick, head of tractor and harvester production, knew just where to look for it: 1,000-plus miles due east of Deere headquarters. McCormick took a train to New York City, where he met a man who was to become one of Deere & Company's most famous resources: industrial designer Henry Dreyfuss.

A New York engineering designer, Dreyfuss reportedly had never heard of John Deere until McCormick first approached him in his Madison Avenue office, with an idea and some background on the Midwestern business. McCormick understood the way farmers thought and felt about their ways of life and doing business on the farm. He

likely shared with Dreyfuss that everything one farmer did for an entire year resulted in only one harvest. And if that farmer were lucky, he'd see maybe 30 or 40 growing seasons in his whole lifetime. That's only a few handfuls of chances to get it right, and a farmer isn't going to waste his chances, or his money, on equipment he can't be proud of just to look at.

Just as Dreyfuss had redesigned the telephone, he would shape Deere's products into merchandise with mass appeal. He immediately accepted McCormick's offer and went to work for the Waterloo manufacturer in August 1937.

Dreyfuss' approach was simple but irrefutable: form follows function follows farm life. If Dreyfuss could improve the utility and safety of the tractor, its ease of maintenance, cost of production, general sales appeal, and overall appearance, he would succeed in meeting the needs of farmers and Deere dealers.

Obvious changes to the leading models A and B included narrower gas tanks and radiator cowlings as well as strip-vented

A low-to-the-hood air intake and an outboard exhaust were two variations of the Model A Regular that made the orchard As popular throughout tree cropping states of the South and West. With a more merciful design for farmers working around delicate, low-hanging citrus branches, some of the tractors wore deep-skirted fenders that covered the rear wheels almost entirely to the ground.

radiator grilles rather than the grid or heavy mesh used previously. These changes improved all-around ground visibility. Curving sheet metal to mold the tractor instead of bolting it squarely into place gave the body a smoother, more streamlined appearance.

Deere engineers had some streamlining of their own in mind when they enhanced the orchard line of Model AO. They modified the tree-guarding body with a V-shaped radiator grille as well as flywheel and pulley guards, they enclosed the air intake and muffler under the hood, and they vented the exhaust to the side (and even piped it below the engine in some examples). Deere renamed the AO-variation Model AOS, using "S" for "streamlined." Nearly 90 Model AOS tractors were built from late 1936 through late 1940, using separate serial numbers from the AO because of the multitude of new parts.

Streamlined didn't mean the same as "styled" in Deere tractors, though. Dreyfuss-styled As and Bs were reinvented front to back. In addition to shaping the front end, Dreyfuss aligned the air intake and exhaust stacks on the hood for clearer straight-ahead vision. Behind the tractor, Dreyfuss rearranged the power takeoff and hydraulic fittings for faster operator recognition and greater ease in hooking up attachments.

Farmers frequently needed to stand at the helm, so Dreyfuss adjusted the seat for better sitting posture and standing room. The old instrument panel was bothersome to read during rough rides through fields, so a more visually coherent control board took its place in style.

By 1941, both the styled Model A and the styled Model B had bigger engines, six-speed transmissions with high-low

Around 820 fixed-tread AOS models were built from 1936–1940. Although the "S" stood for streamlined, these tractors certainly had a style all their own, including V-shaped radiator guards unlike any other Deere design.

shift levers, electric starts, and front and rear belt-generated lights. But to meet the buying demands of skeptical farmer-patrons, Deere continued manufacturing upgrades of existing and new unstyled models for years. The latter appealed to farmers who didn't trust a new look in the tractor that they expected to replace their current proven one.

In the middle of the decade, old and new Deere tractors already looked ages apart. Deere downshifted production on all its mature models. By decade's end, the company had outlived its old-fashioned but never-to-be obsolete green-and-yellow originals. The unstyled Deere tractor settled into its place in history.

Like the other early As, the Model AOS had a 5.5x6.5-inch bore and stroke engine and ran at 975 rpm. In 1940 it was replaced with a larger engined AO model.

Chapter 5

DOWN-TO-EARTH MOVERS

Models G, H, L, LA, and M Are Driven by Producers, not Mass-Producers

Mechanization during the Roaring Twenties lifted the farmer to a new agricultural high, just as the Depression had dragged him to the ground. As a result of those desolate years, the agricultural economy had been divided into the haves and have-nots.

Those who had the acreage and dependable markets in which to sell their crops also had the big machines to plow, plant, cultivate, and harvest. Those who had not still did the heavy labor with a couple of horses and as much manpower as it took to drive, feed, and care for the team.

The Model L was unique in many ways from prior models. The 1938 "unstyled" model (pictured here) used a Ford Model A three-speed transmission with a Hercules upright two-cylinder engine. Note the tubular chassis that slopes downward from front to rear. The large gap between engine and operator provides an unusual look and masks the tractor's short overall length of 91 inches.

Both sets of farmers wanted more, though. The well-off producers desired more power and versatility than the heavy-duty Models D, GP, and A could provide, even as Henry Dreyfuss' styling was improving operator efficiency, safety, and satisfaction. The smaller farmers still needed a push to go into town and buy a tractor. They wanted the ideal tractor for them, one not too big and, more important, not too costly to

FARMERS WAIT FOR THE DUST TO SETTLE

Farmers weren't the only ones who knew the severity of the topsoil erosion that plagued the agricultural world during the 1930s. Appointed by Roosevelt in 1933 as the secretary of agriculture, the outspoken Henry A. Wallace was well aware of the situation.

He attributed the vast loss of soil nutrients to more than just the economy and environment. In a February 1940 article entitled "The War at Our Feet," which was published in the social-political journal *Survey Graphic,* the soon-to-be-vice-president Wallace blamed the governed structure of farming for the long-term detriment of once fertile land.

"For one thing, and this is important in our West especially, the government gave out land 'on the square'—in an enlargement of the gridiron pattern of our wrongly laid out cities and towns. There are not many par of even flat land that can be farmed on the square and the soil remain stable," Wallace wrote.

Beyond suggesting improvements in efficiency, he pointed to the available technology, such as tractors, as a saving grace to agriculture from over-cropping during World War I. "Today we not only know better, [but] we have new equipment; we have machine equipment. It has helped tear soil down, but may also be turned. We see now to the task of defense, to build soil up again."

Conserving America's natural resources, including farmland, was becoming a heartfelt issue with farmers for the first time in the country's soil-rich history. Wallace tugged at the heartstrings of rural Americans to defend their soils, even as World War II loomed. "Here and there," he continued, "farmers have already joined in a new combination and a new field pattern of culture. Farms that used to resemble storehouses laid end to end now lock together in swirls. They sprawl on the earth securely. It is a striking design, dictated by the earth's conformation and as individual to a given stretch of country as a human fingerprint.

"The basic agricultural idea is to get away from square farming in a round country. The main thing is to reform fields and rotations into strip-patterns, cut to the curve of the land, much as the parts of a garment are cut to the configuration of a human body."

It was a serious topic for farmers of all regional, social, and financial strata. Between in 1934 and 1939, 35 million erosion-claimed acres of farmland had become 57 million acres of unusable farmland. For all these reasons, the desire for a more economical, more efficient, and more farm-friendly tractor grew even stronger. And Deere & Company would have to build such a machine if it would reach the fragile fields of late 1930s America.

justify getting rid of their beloved horses and mules. As configurable as it was, Deere's nearly two-ton $700 baby B was still too large and expensive.

Making the decision to invest in their land by purchasing machinery became even more difficult for farmers as topsoil erosion problems became serious in the Midwest, South, and West. The overscraping and overforaging of surplus-producing croplands and pastures that were desperately plowed, harvested, and grazed during the early 1930s, combined with extensive mid-1930s droughts, eventually caused the Dust Bowl effect, starving much farmland of its integrity. So in order to prevent whatever land they had from becoming a wasteland, farmers had to adjust their cultivating and harvesting methods.

LIFE IN THE FIELDS BECOMES A LITTLE EASIER

Deere & Company already had intentions of building a tractor for every farmer at that time. The dozen-plus variations of its smallest tractor to date, the Model B, reflected the company's goal to fit every type of farm. But the smallest and most stubborn farmers still weren't buying tractors. The holdouts became Deere's new target market.

For the first and last time since the beginning of the twentieth century, on-farm population actually increased from 1930 to 1940, by nearly 400,000 people. The percentage of career farmers was still on its steady, fateful decline, however, and now represented less than a fifth of the country's total workforce.

During the Dust Bowl devastation, field hands in the South's Cotton Belt, the Midwest's Corn Belt, and other areas shuffled off farms to find work elsewhere. Some migrated west and entered mining or logging camps; others found work in towns and cities where office and industrial jobs were scarce but advantageous. By the end of the Depression in the late

1930s, round-the-clock farm laborers had a taste of factory pay and 60-hour-or-less work weeks. There was no need to return to the farm, not even when the rains came and the grass grew greener.

The small farmers who remained needed to keep up with technology to compete for their shrinking market shares. Family farms were losing out on markets and contracts to processors, as larger producers and newly formed corporate farms began to flourish. But Deere & Company intended to keep every farmer up to speed with technology through its

A styled Model L from 1946, the last production year. The L was a one-plow tractor, built to win over the small farm operator who might still be relying on a team of two horses or mules to handle planting and plowing.

NEBRASKA TEST No. 313 (1938)

Tractor model	Y, 62, and L
Production years	1937–1942
Serial numbers	621000–642038
Drawbar rating (hp)	7.01
Belt pulley/PTO rating (hp)	9.27
Fuel	gasoline
Only 26 Model Y prototypes and 78 Model 62s were made. The eventual Model L also had an industrial version, Model LI.	

NEBRASKA TEST No. 373 (1941)	
Tractor model	LA
Production years	1940–1946
Serial numbers	1001–13475
Drawbar rating (hp)	10.46
Belt Pulley/PTO rating (hp)	12.93
Fuel	gasoline
LA industrial versions were not given a separate letter model designation.	

amalgamation of tractor lines. The board's latest decision was to build a smaller, lighter-weight, more all-purpose machine than even the flexible Model B. And the company didn't want to bog the project down in its experimental department in Waterloo, where Theo Brown had bigger tractors to create.

In 1936, veering from its normal course of tractor design, the company kept the unassuming, one-plow project at home in Moline. Using the talents of Ira Maxon, chief engineer and manager of Deere's wagon works, the manufacturer began rendering production Model Y—the tractor for America's smallest farms.

Maxon enlisted the engineering assistance of his old friend Willard Nordenson to design and develop the engine

The "styled" tractors incorporated curves and flowing lines, creating a more integrated look. This 1941 Model LA has a Deere gasoline engine that puts out close to 13 horsepower at the drawbar.

power for Model Y. Initially, the team devised a tractor that used an upright-mounted two-cylinder, with its crankshaft parallel to the tractor's direction of travel. The engineers promoted the longitude-oriented engine as a visibility enhancement for single-row crop work.

The gasoline-only, 8-horsepower Novo C-66 lasted only a short time in design because of mechanical breakdowns in its main bearing and crankshaft as well as its limited lubricating ability. After fewer than two dozen prototypes, Maxon and Nordenson switched to an upright twin 3x4-inch Hercules NXA, which was built to Deere specifications. This engine became their power source for nearly 1,600 tractors—additional Ys in 1936, which later became Model 62s in 1937 and were the first Model Ls. These remained unstyled through 1938.

Other elements favorable to the eventual Model L included an H-shift transmission, adapted from the popular Model A Ford car. Budget concerns notwithstanding, the Model L designers had a plan to promote the simplicity of L's three-speed driving ease and maneuverability. This new one-man tractor was intended for the farm, naturally, but it would work just as well on a golf course, on a lawn, and even in cemetery maintenance. The L's versatility also led to industrial utility, and bright yellow LIs were built alongside their John Deere–green counterparts.

Used mainly for light jobs around warehouses, shops, and work yards, the L's stocky frame—shortened by nearly 30 inches from the original Model B chassis—made the weight distribution important to both the tractor's safety and operation. Offsetting the engine and steering a little to the left and seating the driver slightly to the right of the centerline balanced the design. The driver steered with his left hand or at an odd angle with his right.

As early as 1937, Dreyfuss had a hand in styling the Model L. Dreyfuss did more than just coif the Model L with an orderly outward appearance. He tended to every func-

T he Model LA was 2 inches longer than the L, at 93 inches overall. Like its slightly smaller sibling, the LA had an engine and steering that were offset to the driver's left—an engineering necessity that Deere claimed improved forward visibility.

tional detail, and countless modifications went to Moline for approval through 1938, including increasing the engine to a 3.25x4-inch Hercules NXB. Months later, the internally named Model 67 was ready, and just in time for the 1939 model year. Unlike every other John Deere tractor that had simultaneous production runs, the birth of the styled L abruptly ended the lifespan of its unstyled predecessor.

Eventually, John Deere's own vertical two-cylinder made its way under the Model L's hood, but the L's 1,200-pound pull didn't give others in the market segment the payoff that they

needed from a small farm tractor, even with a price tag of less than $500. So in 1941, a stronger, comparably priced Model LA went to market. Its 3.5x4-inch John Deere L-head vertical engine sent 50 percent more power to the LA's near-one-ton-maximum field tow rating. The engine also carried power to the electric starter and lights, which were optional along with the generator and batteries.

As promised, the garden-variety one-plow models L and LA were versions born from Deere's quality big-iron lineage. Now there was a Deere tractor for every size farm.

Deere built 235 of its Hi-Crop Model G, nearly half of which were exported. This design was slated to be Model F, but International Harvester was already on the market with their Farmall F, so Deere skipped ahead one letter. The overhead steering was paired with a shorter radiator in early production, but overheating problems led Deere to incorporate the larger unit used on this 1953 model.

This shot highlights the tall stance of the Model G Hi-Crop. Though built to straddle taller crops, the high-seated tractor had another benefit: fewer mosquitoes reached the operator. The padded seat with backrest was another plus for those who spent long hours at the wheel.

NEBRASKA TEST No. 295 (1937)

Tractor model	G (early)
Production years	1938–1941
Serial numbers	1000–12192
Drawbar rating (hp)	20.70
Belt pulley/PTO rating (hp)	31.44
Fuel	distillate (run)/gasoline (start)

The U.S.'s entrance into World War II in December 1941 contributed to Deere & Company's efficient redesign of the G, which was an improved six-speed version of the original. The "modernized" G was aptly labeled the GM. Its first run lasted only months before production went on a wartime hold with serial number 13747. The tractor manufacturing and GM serial numbers picked up where they left off in October 1944 with model GM number 13748.

Proportioned like a smaller Model G—shorter in height and length and narrower—the Model H was a general purpose row-crop tractor with a single-plow capability. It was less expensive than the G and closer to the L in power. This is a 1941 HWH. The latter two letters in the model stand for wide, high-clearance.

GARNISH WITH A HELPING OF G AND H

With its basics covered and niche markets filled, Deere decided it was time for farmers to upgrade their tractors. After all, not every farmer suffered the worst of the Depression. Some farms even prospered in the late 1930s, and those operators were ready to sample the new and improved industrial farm-power technology.

First, the company focused on beefing up its main course of general-purpose farm tractors with a machine like models D, A, and B. As a full three-plow version of the A and B design, the Model G was a true successor.

Deere advertised its unstyled Model G in a 1941 brochure as being, "in most other respects" than power, "identical to Models 'A' and 'B,' previously described—tractors that have met the most exacting needs of row-crop farmers in all sections of the country."

Built first in May 1937, Model G had a 6.125x7-inch horizontal I-head engine. Its original 20.70-drawbar horsepower and 31.44 belt horsepower gave the tractor mammoth strength to pull more than two tons.

The G two-wheeled tricycle was more powerful than the Model D but 1,000 pounds lighter and bore the most similarity to a row-crop Model A. Though the two tractors produced the same 975 rpm engine speed, the Johnny A's and Johnny G's "poppin'" sounds differed slightly because of the latter's larger bore and stroke.

The big G's low-to-the-ground 11-gallon radiator ran hot—too hot for most warmer-climate fields—and Deere had to recall more than 2,500 of its original models for a taller retrofitted radiator to better cool the massive engine. The subsequent 10,000-plus unstyled G models had 2-gallon-larger radiators, reshaped with an indention in the hood to allow the overhead steering shaft ample clearance.

The United States was fully engaged in World War II by the time the G received its styling treatment from Dreyfuss. But wartime rationing of manufacturing materials

The Model H had three forward gears, with a maximum forward speed of just under 6 miles per hour. Reverse speed topped out at 1.75 miles per hour. The Model H yielded about 12.50 drawbar and just under 15 PTO/belt horsepower.

NEBRASKA TEST No. 383 (1947)	
Tractor model	G (late)
Production years	1941–1953
Serial numbers	13000–64530
Drawbar rating (hp)	27.01
Belt pulley/PTO rating (hp)	33.83
Fuel	All-Fuel
The modernized Model GM went back to being called just Model G for the 1947 production year.	

T he California Hi-Crop HWH was built only in 1941. This photo highlights the Model H's overhead steering and the high-crop variation's axle extensions.

forced Deere to scale back its ideas on rubber tires and running improvements, such as six-speed transmissions and an electric starter.

To avoid missing out on sales from Henry Dreyfuss' improved design, company executives cleverly distinguished the new version as "modernized" and officially reclassified the tractor as a Model GM. Deere sold more than 9,000 GMs by the end of the war, when it dropped the M characteristics in

1947 and resumed production with styled Gs at a hefty price increase—to $1,879 from the pre-war $1,185.

Next in line alphabetically was the last tractor to make it to market before the onset of the war—the Model H. Pushed into production hurriedly with the Model G, the Model H filled a final gap between mid-sized and small row-crop machines.

Deere even billed the H as the perfect second tractor for bigger farmers with large vegetable gardens. With a

NEBRASKA TEST No. 312 (1938)	
Tractor model	H
Production years	1939–1947
Serial numbers	1000–61116
Drawbar rating (hp)	9.68
Belt pulley/PTO rating (hp)	12.97
Fuel	distillate (run)/gasoline (start)
Includes variations HNH (later known as California Hi-Crops model), HW, and HWH.	

OUR COUNTRY AT WAR, OUR COMPANY AT WORK

In August 1942, nearly 1,000 Deere & Company employees from across the United States answered the call by their company leadership: They decided to serve their country and "Join the John Deere Battalion." Recruitment posters printed in red, white, and blue helped spur the recruitment effort as factory workers, branch mechanics, and dealers signed up for wartime military service. Deere headquartered its effort on the third floor of the company's general offices at 1325 3rd Avenue in Moline, Illinois, and those who joined became part of a special group within the U.S. Army.

Initially, the five companies that made up the battalion were officially named the 303 Ordnance Regiment. This group of 624 enlisted Deere men from 48 states eventually became the 608th Ordnance Base Armament Maintenance Battalion.

After basic training on the East Coast, the battalion received advanced training on the West Coast and learned General George Patton's tank maneuvers in the Californian desert sands before heading back East. They left for war on November 3, 1943, and crossed the Atlantic in only five days. They traveled to Scotland in the largest passenger liner of the day, the Queen Elizabeth. The ship sailed alone, and the Deere men were packed aboard the boat with 18,000 troops from all parts of the military. The soldiers slept three deep on makeshift canvas bunks, with not even enough room to change clothes or eat sitting down during the week-long voyage.

According to the November 25, 1942, issue of Deere's in-house newsletter, the *Bugle Call Rag*, the mechanical and trade skills of the John Deere Battalion were first class. The troops were "especially qualified for maintenance work on tanks, combat cars, armored vehicles, field artillery, small arms, and fire control instruments."

From its landing near Glasgow, the John Deere Battalion made its way to Warminster, England, where its mission was made clear—to overhaul, test, and prepare Patton's tanks for "Operation Overlord." The group's work was integral to the

★ ★ ★ ★ ★ ★ ★ ★ ★ ★ ★ ★ ★ ★ ★ ★ ★ ★ ★

JOIN THE
JOHN DEERE BATTALION
U. S. ARMY

The War Department has asked the John Deere organization to form a U. S. Army Battalion for service as a maintenance unit for keeping mechanized combat equipment in operation. Men will be recruited from John Deere factories, branch houses, and dealers' stores.

The John Deere Maintenance Battalion offers an unusual opportunity to both single and married employees, from 18 to 45 years of age, who expect to enter military service soon or later. The advantages to be obtained by joining are as follows:

1. An opportunity to enter the service with fellow John Deere employees—men you already know and with whom you have worked.

2. It offers the very unusual opportunity for you to use your mechanical skill and knowledge in the military service—to continue your training and development in useful and profitable after-war occupations.

3. The work of maintenance battalions such as John Deere is organizing includes many jobs requiring special skill and special training. Higher pay is provided for the men assigned to these jobs. If the battalion is assigned to foreign service, its members will receive an additional 20% increase in pay.

Act Today

All John Deere men have an equal opportunity to qualify for the John Deere Battalion and for its special jobs, but early completion of enlistments is urgent. If you expect to enter military service any time in the future, see or write your Factory or Branch House Manager—today—for further information about the unusual opportunities which this John Deere Maintenance Battalion may have for you.

★ ★ ★ ★ ★ ★ ★ ★ ★ ★ ★ ★ ★ ★ ★ ★ ★ ★ ★

Nearly 1,000 direct Deere & Company employees first answered the call to join the military by serving in the company's special John Deere Battalion branch of the U.S. Army. *Deere & Company Archives*

operation, which came to fruition on June 5, 1944. The invasion of the more than 150,000 troops at Normandy Beach in France was better known back home as D-day.

On the frontlines, every minute that ticked off the clock was a mark of continuing survival for the soldiers. And during heightened battles, every soldier was prepared for the possibility of being cut-off from the rest of his company. Although the John Deere Battalion served behind "the front," the group was no less prepared to survive.

The many talents of the men made the battalion's companies versatile enough to handle any day-to-day jobs, as well as the more taciturn military assignments. "Everything from cooks to watch repairmen," the company newsletter touted, "In order to be complete in itself and also capable of meeting any emergency."

As a whole, the soldiers who trained stateside in North Carolina and California served tours of duty mainly in England and France before going to Belgium at the end of the Allied forces' combat in the European Theater. Small detachments of the John Deere Battalion went other places on special assignment or on top-secret missions during the height of the war and before the Pacific campaign ended with Japan's surrender in 1945. After 40 months of existence, the battalion disbanded. In that time, its members had spent only a little more than two years in the eastern hemisphere.

Back in the United States, during the early years of the war, Deere & Company made a full-fledged commitment to producing materials for the U.S. Navy and War Department. In 1942 and 1943, the tractor giant made more than $168 million in equipment and parts for the ongoing battles overseas, including 2,190 of its own MG-1 military tractors, which were based on the "modernized" Model G design. At least 11 of the Deere & Company factories that were operational during the war helped build the MG fleet. Most of the factories produced the parts; some built and tested transmissions while others made the side frames. Another Deere factory handled the final manufacturing. Later, Deere referred to its in-house collaboration as "a 'family' job from start to finish."

No matter what the scale of production, the U.S. government mandated that all wartime contractors fulfill their roles as efficiently as possible. Deere & Company stringently squeezed every drop of economical output possible from its factories, equip-

As a military subcontractor, Deere & Company employed many Americans back home in building everything from laundry units to tank and aircraft parts. At the Dain Manufacturing Company, in Ottumwa, Iowa, one Deere woman works to assemble the tail wheel for a P-47 fighter plane during World War II. *Deere & Company Archives*

ment, and materials, as well as its employees. It was no easy task for anyone in the company—from the factory worker to the executive—to adjust to the new environment, as Deere & Company wrote in its 1950 corporate report Deere & Company in Peace and War:

"It was soon discovered by Company officials that in tackling a job so unrelated to building farm implements, manufacturing know-how depended less on the product than on the processes used in making it. Also, another influencing factor is the state of mind of the personnel; they must accept the new processes promptly and organize production to accommodate them."

Sometimes Deere was only the assembler of the necessary military equipment, but even those jobs carried with them a gigantic learning curve for workers. For example, the mobile laundry units that were used by U.S. troops required Deere's effective scheduling of the more than 2,000 separate parts to be put together into just one finished product.

Outside of its factory walls, Deere and & Company urged its customers to show their patriotism by living as shrewdly as possible. Its advertising department created a lot of literature encouraging maximized crop production and minimized waste. The company emphatically took up federal causes at great monetary expense, even campaigning for gasoline conservation and for non-farm families to grow Victory Gardens. "Eat what you can, and can what you can't eat," went the slogan.

Deere had always reused its own byproducts, but now it diligently collected everything salvageable, recycling all aluminum, brass, copper, iron, lead, rubber, steel, tin, and zinc to shore up the war effort. The company urged farmers with old equipment to turn in their rusty, broken-downs as scrap. And farmers did.

Deere's official publication, *The Furrow*, expressed the sentiments of the company and the nation in one scrap drive write-up: "It may be junk to you. But it keeps our steel mills running, helps build tanks, ships, and planes, helps fire our guns, and drop bombs on Tokio [*sic*] and Berlin."

Deere employees were just as committed to the war effort—90 percent of Deere & Company workers from six of its factories and eight branch locations accepted at least 10 percent of their paychecks in U.S. War Bonds during those years.

By the end of WWII, nearly 4,900 Deere & Company employees—more than one-third of the company's entire workforce—offered their bravery and sacrifice to serve the military in some capacity. Of those who returned from foreign soils, more than 600 were back to work by October 1945. Soon thereafter, Deere & Company enacted plans to return no fewer than 350 employees per month.

The last of the John Deere Battalion men came home to New York Harbor on New Year's Day 1946.

yard of adjustable rear tread width—from 44 inches up to 80 inches—and three speeds, the Model H had the advantage as a one-plow machine. For about $600, farmers got a whole 12 inches more range of tread width than with a Model B and 600 pounds more pull than with an L. The Model H's design quickly lent it to other variations, including the wide-high (HWH), narrow (HN), and narrow high-clearance (HNH).

Running on cheap distillate fuels during times of petroleum rationing certainly didn't hurt sale of the Model H lines, which reached a total production of 58,263, despite a couple of factory stops and starts throughout the war.

MAKE MINE A DEERE

As the war neared its end, Deere was ready to get back to the business of producing tractors full time. In addition to losing production space for farm equipment to fabrication of artillery shell casings, military tractors, airplane parts, and other war-related goods, Deere & Company sent more than 4,500 enlisted employees into service. In the meantime, the company had been working hard at home to maintain its place in the tractor market.

Since 1939, Deere had sold about 25,000 tractors to the small-farmer target audience it had so aggressively tried to woo with crop- and task-specific variations of several single- and two-plow models. But Deere's entire lineup was no match for the return of Henry Ford and his new partner, Harry Ferguson.

Together, Ford and Ferguson developed an N series of wide-front, standard-tread tractors with a three-point hitch system that gave the farmers what they most coveted—power. The Ford-Ferguson 9N outsold and outperformed Deere's B, L, LA, and H models by 50 percent. Through the end of the war, Ford's only tractor offering sold on average 17,000 more units than Deere's small fleet each year.

Deere wanted to downsize the multitude of parts it built

The Model M was designed to compete with Henry Ford's N-series tractors. The standard M wore Deere's traditional green and yellow paint scheme. This is an M industrial model, or MI. The four-speed Model M was good for 10 to 12 miles per hour.

NEBRASKA TEST Nos. 387 (1947)/423 (1949 Model MT)/448 (1950 Model MC)	
Tractor model	M
Production years	1947–1952
Serial numbers	10001–50580
Drawbar rating (hp)	14.39/14.08/13.70
Belt pulley/PTO rating (hp)	18.21/18.33/18.89
Fuel	gasoline or All-Fuel

Deere built a new factory in Dubuque, Iowa, for its production of the Model M and its variations, including the MC, MI, MT, MTN, and MTW.

The Model MC, a Model M crawler, was conceived at Deere's new plant in Dubuque, Iowa. But it was developed by Jesse Lindeman at the Lindeman Power Equipment Company in Yakima, Washington. Important the Model M's success was the Quick-Tatch implement attachment system, which saved farmers a tremendous amount of time in securing and removing machinery.

The MC crawler used an upright, inline two-cylinder gasoline or an all-fuel engine with electric start. Twelve-inch-wide track shoes were standard, though Deere offered 10- and 14-inch shoes as well. This 1952 MC is all Deere, the company having bought out the Lindemans late in 1946.

and increase its sale of tractors at the same time. The company's board agreed to buy a new plant that would accommodate an upswing in production. By 1946, Deere & Company had moved into a new town: Dubuque, Iowa.

The first assembly project at the Dubuque Tractor Works was a totally different Deere tractor that was actually born in Moline. It was called the Model M, and its 1947 debut was the company's answer to Ford's N.

The Model M rolled the best of models L, LA, and H together so that Deere could retire the lot. Designed as a general-purpose utility tractor, Model M was powered by gasoline and Deere's seldom-used vertical L-head two-cylinder engine, with a 4x4-inch bore and stroke and high-speed 1,650-rpm output.

Its size and strength made the M well suited for several different farm applications, including harvesting specialty crops. In its effort to make all markets Deere markets, the manufacturer configured its MT with an adjustable-width front and offered two- and one-wheel versions. With more than a few differences up front, the Model M had another

option that Ford couldn't match: Touch-O-Matic independent left and right aft hydraulic implement lifts. Touch-O-Matic lifts ran off the crankshaft, so farmers could set the working depth even at a standstill before taking off through the field, thereby lessening the chance for error. By controlling implements individually, the farmer could more precisely work his fields when rounding a corner or some other obstacle, such as a pond or stubborn patch of thistle.

Deere also became its own crawler manufacturer during this era, leaving Jesse Lindeman's models behind. The first-ever Deere-designed crawler tractor, the MC, made tracks in 1949. Later that same year, the MI went to work off the farm in coats of Industrial Yellow or Highway Orange paint.

As a matter of power, the M was a valiant and viable effort but, in the end, a vain attempt on Deere's part to overtake Ford-Ferguson's new 8N. In the model's five-year lifespan at Deere, the famous carmaker and his Irish designer tromped Moline's 87,000-unit sales of all Model M versions five times over.

Chapter 6

ENTER THE DIESEL

An Increasing Need for Power Fuels the Model R

Times weren't changing; they were already changed by the beginning of the 1950s. The vast majority of farmers had electricity and cars, and nearly half had telephones. Of course, a mainstay in mechanical farm work was the tractor, which plowed, sowed, cultivated, and harvested in a force two million strong across America.

Strength was the No. 1 need of farmers after World War II. Many had permanently lost their field helpers, including hired hands, sons, and other family to overseas battles or city-slicker jobs. Draft animals, too, were waning as a source of farm power. Farmers rarely replaced

Previous pages

The Model R was Deere's first diesel tractor. The company had experimented with diesel going back into the 1930s, but it had not seriously pursued the technology. As a result its competitors were stealing sales as maximum power became essential.

workhorses and mules that died and sometimes sold their equine teams for other livestock when a tractor purchase was more fitting for the farm.

Kerosene wasn't as cheap a fuel source for farmers as it had been early in the century. Faster, high-compression engine–powered vehicles had become commonplace on and off the farm. These cars, trucks, tractors, and buses skyrocketed both driver and passenger demand for gasoline. The demand in turn raised prices for kerosene, which was made of the same petroleum products as mainstream gasoline.

Grudgingly, farmers shelled out more money to keep their tractors rolling. They were also realizing—from firsthand wartime experiences driving four- and six-cylinder military vehicles and diesel crawlers—that more engine power was available than they had back home in their traditional two-cylinder tractors. Wheat and rice farmers, especially, needed bigger machines to farm their increasingly vast areas of cropland.

Economies of scale and the ever-increasing farmer demands for more power finally pushed Deere to jump feet-first into a move the company had considered for years: creating a diesel John Deere tractor.

Cooling the Model R's huge two-cylinder diesel engine requires a powerful fan. Out in the fields, this fan draws dust and debris into the radiator mesh. The corrugations in the mesh are designed for easy cleaning by a farmer's gloved hand. The tractor's stout look is no deception. It tips the scales at about 7,500 pounds.

This 1949 R had meaty tires and considerable horsepower for its day. It pulled more than three tons at its maximum.

NEBRASKA TEST No. 406 (1949)	
Tractor model	R Diesel
Production years	1949–1954
Serial numbers	1000–22293
Drawbar rating (hp)	34.27
Belt pulley/PTO rating (hp)	43.32
Fuel	diesel (run)/gasoline (start)

With its 5.75x8-inch diesel engine, the Model R Diesel was Deere's biggest—its radiator towered over 6.5 feet— and most powerful two-cylinder engine to date. Here, the 45 horsepower goliath sows the vast grain fields of Great Falls, Montana, with a Van Brunt drill. *Deere & Company Archives*

GO AHEAD, EVERYBODY ELSE IS DOING IT

New fuel sources were hard to come by in the mid-twentieth century. The tractor market had explored its few options: distillates, gasoline, and diesel. Since the early 1930s, gasoline-start diesel tractors had captured a stronghold in the crawler market. The first diesel tractor, the Caterpillar Diesel 65, had made Caterpillar a household name. The tractor used a pony motor to warm up its diesel engine. Next to make diesel history was Deere's rival, International Harvester, also using the pony motor in its WD-40 to sell the first diesel-powered tractor on wheels.

About the same time the competition secured their boundaries in the diesel machine market, Deere was staking a claim. Since the mid-1930s, the company's leading engineers had had a directive from the top to get diesel units into testing, and they did. But in creating a tractor that swayed from Deere's traditional dual gasoline-powered cylinders, the company inevitably created an industry hullabaloo that its tractor blueprint was in transformation. And the days of the two-cylinder tractor were numbered. Switching to the diesel concept for more power meant using an altogether different engine design, which was a foreign concept to those at Deere.

A steel cab was an appealing option for Model R purchasers. This 1950 Model shows how the cab offered relief from sun, as well as rain. The hinged windows provided excellent ventilation.

In the end, Deere & Company engineers had to modify their two-cylinder design to get a working diesel. After trying different starters on different engines, the two-cylinder pony motor proved the best approach to getting a two-cylinder diesel warmed up enough to start.

In 1940, the first prototype Deere diesels went into the works. From 1941 through 1945, the first eight MX experimental models received rigorous field-testing in Texas, Arizona, and Minnesota. During that time, concentrated redevelopment of the MX led to five new models. Continuous fine-tuning led two years later to the final MX version, the immediate predecessor to Deere's first marketable diesel. Finally that day dawned on January 12, 1949, when Deere released its last alpha-series tractor—the Model R, serial number 1000.

I n cold weather, diesel fuel becomes like jelly, compounding the problem of starting a high-compression diesel engine. The gasoline pony engine that helped start the Model R warmed both the fuel and engine block beforehand. The Model R was the last of Deere's lettered tractors.

Using an electric starter, the Model R's 2.6x2.3-inch gasoline pony engine ran 4,000 rpm and fired up enough exhaust heat to thin the thick diesel fuel in cold weather, thereby making its ignition as simple as pulling a lever. And the R was as mighty as it was massive. Meant to give farmers a modern, more powerful replacement for their beloved Model D, the R could pull five 14-inch plows all day long with its one main 22-gallon tank of diesel. The same amount of work would have taken Grandfather D two days and almost twice as much fuel. The R's large 5.75x8-inch horizontal I-head engine drove 1,000 rpm. By comparison, a new 1949 Model D with its 6.75x7-inch horizontal L-head engine ran at 900 rpm. The R produced nearly 50 percent more maximum pulling power than the D, rating 34.27 drawbar horsepower and 43.32 horsepower at the belt in its Nebraska Test. It was 50 percent bigger and cost more than twice as much, too. With such might, the five-speed R secured its place in the company's standard-tread hall of fame as the toughest letter in the Deere alphabet.

Operator-friendly features were part of what drove the Model R's mass appeal. Deere put its strongest face forward in Henry Dreyfuss' Model R masterpiece design, which went unchanged during the tractor's whole five-year, 21,000-plus

An extra set of rear wheels reduces ground compaction by distributing the tractor's weight over a greater area. More tread on the ground will also improve traction, especially on soft ground.

The 416-ci diesel offered ample power, but presented its own challenge. With 16:1 compression, it was no easy powerplant to set in motion. Deere solved the problem with a 10 horsepower gasoline-fueled starting engine. The Moline works contributed the 23-ci starting engine, drawing on experience in manufacturing the small Model Y, L, and LA engines.

production span. The imposing, vertically corrugated grille distinguished the Model R from previous Dreyfuss styles, but it towered with a purpose. Because the huge cooling fan of the R created formidable suction, the new, more angular, accordion-fold design relieved farmers of having to constantly and meticulously unclog the mesh radiator front. Instead, with a brief stop, a gloved hand could simply sweep away field debris.

The time Deere took to perfect its R was a decade well spent. With the Model R barely into its reign, however, talk again surfaced of the limits of two-cylinder engine power.

ONE BIG DIESEL-POWERED DEBATE

"Here we go again," Deere executives must have thought when rumors of revolt swelled up in the ranks of salesmen. There was no squelching the majority of voices, though, which were clamoring for more power even as Deere's first diesel hauled with Herculean strength.

Deere hadn't made a tractor powered by more than two cylinders since its short-lived Dain All-Wheel Drive in the century's late teens. But the development of the Model R diesel stirred the salesmen, who were always poised to promote the next best thing to their customers.

To make certain no dealer continued the hearsay of future multiple-cylinder tractors, the Minneapolis Deere & Webber branch sent a stern bulletin to its employees in late December 1936. It read, in part, "We are again receiving reports, originating no doubt from competitive tractor salesmen, stating we were coming out with a four-cylinder tractor. . . . WE ARE NOT MAKING A FOUR-CYLINDER TRACTOR, NOR ARE WE EVER THINKING OF MAKING ONE." In fact, the company's own Waterloo Tractor Works manager issued an official Deere & Company factory denial of an increase in cylinder production.

Deere & Company leadership was wary to stray from the two-cylinder engine because the company was hesitant to mess with a good thing. The signature of every John

The Model R had a top speed of 11.5 miles per hour with its five-speed gearbox. Deere made some 21,000 of the Model R between 1949 and 1954. This is a 1949 model.

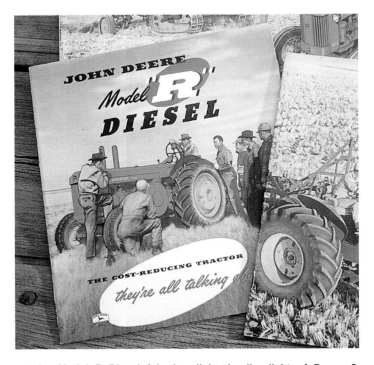

The Model R Diesel faired well in the limelight of Deere & Company literature, based on its sheer size and the magnitude of its proven performance. Deere & Company sold more than 21,000 of its last letter series tractors in just five years. *Nick Cedar*

Deere ignored diesel power for a long time, to its detriment and its competi industrial model from 1952.

Deere tractor was its two-cylinder engine, which 'pop-popped' to the same rhythm in all the Deere tractors and was known for its dependability. Also, Deere had built a great part of its reputation on simplicity of repair—farmers didn't need to be mechanics to fix their tractors. Other

dvantage. When it did jump into the technology, Deere looked at a variety of applications, including an industrial variant. This Model RI is an experimental

makers' four- and six-cylinder machines had more power, but they were harder to maintain.

Still, even with more complicated mechanics, four- and six-cylinder machines were catching attention among farmers. With the increased use of hydraulics, the typical 50-horse-

power two-cylinder engine was no longer powerful enough to get the job done. Yet the glory of Deere's legendary two-cylinder engine would carry through to another milestone in Deere development: a number series.

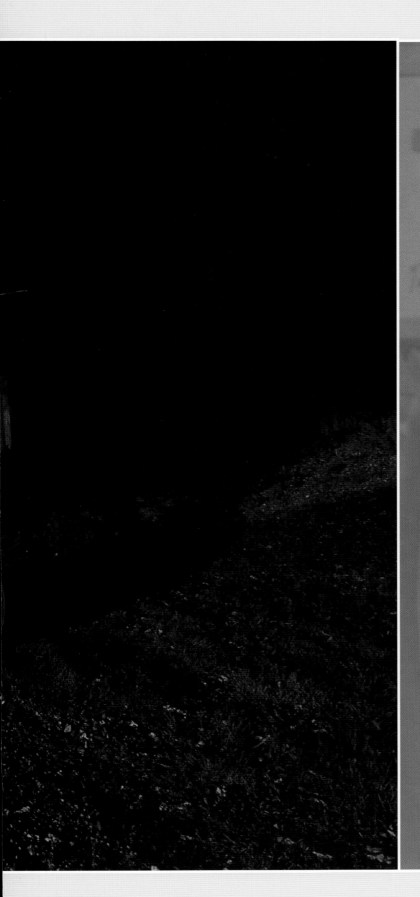

Chapter 7

TWO-CYLINDER DAYS ARE NUMBERED

Letters Yield to 40s Through 80s and the 20- and 30-Series

In creating the number series, Deere & Company still clung to its basic two-cylinder mantra. And because Deere's engine backbone was being preserved, designers sought other ways to improve these tractors. One of their innovations included crafting a precision fuel mixture and intake through separate carburetors, or diesel fuel injectors, for each cylinder. This system gave the engineers increased fuel efficiency and allowed them to squeeze the last drop of horsepower out of Deere's two-cylinder headliner.

For long days in the fields, the Model 70 came standard with lights. Hi-crop models like this one were made from late 1953 to 1956. The 380-ci gasoline engine made 44 horsepower at the drawbar by the end of production.

ON A TEN-SCALE

The renewed-power series of Deere tractors intentionally replaced the production of every model that was left—A through R. Summarily replacing its alphabet, Deere & Company took only four years to produce its entire lineup of new models, numbered in multiples of 10.

The John Deere 60 rolled off the assembly line in March 1952, followed by the 50 in June. Both models were an anti-aging treatment for the old A and B concepts of power and versatility built for every farm. But the improved performance and convenience of the 50 and 60 justified Deere's replacement of its previous line.

Model 50 was the offspring of the smaller B. The biggest performance changes came in horsepower—the 50 doubled the horsepower of the B—and "live" capabilities. "Live" capabilities meant that the 50 had a power takeoff with an individual clutch. So for the first time, engine-powered equipment that ran behind the tractor wasn't affected by the operator's driving functions, such as shifting gears, lifting hydraulic implements, or stopping and starting in transit.

Another revolutionary Deere enhancement to the 50 and 60, as well as subsequent models, was a more aggressive hydraulic system, called Powr-Trol. This live, high-pressure power source also operated separately from both the transmission and power takeoff. Whether built in or attached, hydraulic lifting wasn't affected by other engine-supported functions. Live PTO and Powr-Trol gave Deere tractors an unmistakable advantage—it was another two

The 1954 60 Standard came with power steering and a 12-volt electrical system. It shared many characteristics with the 50 and 70. The 60 provided 37 horsepower at the drawbar, from a 321-ci engine.

Among the various attachments available for the Model 60 was this large circular saw. Machines were simpler then, yet the absence of a safety shield or guard meant operators and their assistants needed to stay alert at all times.

years before International Harvester offered live PTO. International Harvester emulated Deere & Company when it introduced its version of live hydraulics, called Lift-All, in 1954 and then renamed its letter-series tractors series in the numerical hundreds.

The 50s and 60s were upfront about their versatility. Every model came factory-standard with the buyer's choice of front-end assemblies that fit into the tractor's two-piece pedestal mount. Each of the variations was interchangeable

and could be purchased after the original tractor sale. These options included Deere fixed dual wheels, the dual-wheel Roll-O-Matic, or a single front wheel for row cropping. The 38-inch standard wide front or adjustable axles, up to 58 inches, were held in place by four cap screws.

One of the longest-lived features of the 50 and 60 survived on many tractors into the next century: Deere's industry-first, variable rack-and-pinion rear tread. Changing from a 62- to a 97-inch rear tread was now an easy adjustment with an optional

NEBRASKA TEST Nos. 486 (1952)/507 (1953 All-Fuel)/540 (1955 LPG)

Tractor model	50
Production years	1952–1956
Serial numbers	5000001–5033751
Drawbar rating (hp)	20.62/17.42/21.90
Belt pulley/PTO rating (hp)	26.32/21.89/27.45
Fuel	gasoline/All-Fuel/LPG

NEBRASKA TEST Nos. 472 (1952)/490 (1953 All-Fuel)/513 (1953 LPG)

Tractor model	60
Production years	1952–1957
Serial numbers	6000001–6064096
Drawbar rating (hp)	27.71/22.57/28.59
Belt pulley/PTO rating (hp)	35.33/28.27/35.90
Fuel	gasoline/All-Fuel/LPG

Variations on the standard Model 60 included the 60H, 60-O, and 60S.

long axle. An additional option of dished wheels allowed the tractors to straddle up to 104-inch row spacing.

The electrical requirements for better lighting and ignition required a doubling of the battery output, up to 12 volts, in the 50 and 60 series. And the need for efficiency didn't stop at the battery compartment under the driver seat—it went all the way to the rear of the tractor. Exhaust pipes had always been a distraction to farmers, blocking their straight-ahead views, limiting overhead clearance into barns, and forcing them to breathe potent, sometimes asphyxiating fumes. Henry Dreyfuss solved these issues for farmers willing to pay a little extra to get the optional rear exhaust, which routed fuel emissions under the rear axle, behind the tractor—and, more important, away from the driver.

Next in line was Deere's Model 70, introduced in 1953. It originated with a 5.875x7-inch horizontal two-cylinder. Weighing in at three tons, the 70 was everything from 50 and 60 with the bulk of the Model G. Like the 50 and 60 before it, the Model 70 came with six speeds and plenty of fuel options. Deere knew that during unforeseeable petroleum shortages, farmers would use what was most economical and readily available. So the Model 50, 60, and 70 tractors came with the farmer's choice of engine, made to run on the farmer's choice of gasoline, "All-Fuel" variations, or liquefied petroleum gas (LPG).

In 1954, the 70 was made into a diesel and set a fuel efficiency record at its Nebraska Test, recording 17.74 horsepower per hour per gallon. As a diesel row-crop tractor, the Model 70 was Deere's first. The diesel Model R was a standard tractor, with fixed-tread wheels in front, good for wheat and rice fields. But the 70, with its tricycle design, fit neatly between corn and cotton rows.

The offering came just in time for row-crop farmers whose operations were getting bigger every day. The average number of acres per American farm had climbed above 250 in the early 1950s, but irrigated acres had jumped to an astonishing 25 million, quadrupling irrigation levels of the 1920s. Just as the average farm acreage had increased, so had the number of tractors. In fact for the first time in 1954, tractor numbers exceeded the total number of horses and mules on farms that were being used for labor. In less than 50 years, the farmer had completed his evolution from hand laborer to machine operator. And competition among tractor producers was heating up as tractors became more commonplace.

Facing up to industry pressure to offer a Ford-Ferguson–like three-point hitch for its tractors, Deere designed its own 801 Hitch. The preliminary type of Deere three-point hitch transferred the weight from implement draft resistance into downward pressure on the drive wheels. Although the 801 Hitch was adequate, it didn't compare to Ford's, whose patent rights eventually ran out in 1953. Deere didn't adapt its famous hydraulic hitch system, though, for another few years.

The push for on-farm efficiencies went beyond equipment, though. Technology used to produce crops had grown in many aspects, and every farmer reaped the benefits. Proven plant and soil sciences improved fertilizer and nutrient use, and because of these changes five more bushels of wheat grew on every acre in 1950 than did in 1930.

By this time, too, the average farmer was feeding 15.5 people at home and abroad. Maintaining the world food supply was fast becoming the job of the American farmer. As a result, every modern farmer was looking to get the job done at a lesser overall cost in time and resources. With the increasing popularity of merchant credit and government support, debt became a manageable part of doing business, and running a farm became more and more like running a corporation. Tractor manufacturers began looking at farmers more as clients, with whom they wanted to maintain long-term relationships.

Deere & Company couldn't sit back on its laurels after the Model 70, so it matched the other end of its tractor spectrum by introducing the Model 40 in tandem with the 70. The 40 was a remake and redesign of the multi-purpose Model M. Fitted with all the features of the 50 through 70, variations of the small tractor replaced each of its predecessor's versions, with even a much-improved crawler, the 40C.

But big, small, and in-between sized tractors weren't enough to keep Deere's momentum going forward—the company wanted bigger. The only place left to go up was in the redesign of the diesel-driven Model R.

These siblings may look like twins, but they're not. A Model 60 Narrow and Model 70 Narrow shoulder the same load: a Model 22 Cotton Harvester.

In replacing the Model R in 1955, after six years of production, Deere made some significant adjustments in the new Model 80 Diesel. For starters, designers increased the main fuel tank by nearly 50 percent, going from 22 to 32.5 gallons, using an electric fuel gauge to measure its fill. An additional forward drive gear made the 80 into a six-speed. A stronger V-4 pony starter engine, employed first in the 70 Diesel, gave the 80 an additional boost in its 5,500 rpm.

The biggest changes to appear in the 80 Diesel came in the form of engine power. With an astonishing horsepower rating of 61.8 on the drawbar and 67.6 off the belt, totaling up to 7,392 pounds at maximum pull, the 80 was a true giant

NEBRASKA TEST Nos. 493 (1953)/506 (1953 All-Fuel)/514 (1953 LPG)	
Tractor model	70
Production years	1953–1956
Serial numbers	7000001–7043757
Drawbar rating (hp)	33.16/30.75/34.58
Belt pulley/PTO rating (hp)	42.80/38.22/44.17
Fuel	gasoline/All-Fuel/LPG
Variations on the Model 70 general purpose tractor included the 70H, 70N, 70S, and 70W.	

The fenders on this styled Model 60 give it an aerodynamic look. Their purpose is not to cheat the wind, but rather the branches this orchard model worked below and between.

in the kingdom of tractors. The bore was increased to 6.125 inches on the signature horizontal two-cylinder engine. For all its increased power, the new diesel weighed only 450 pounds more, and it cost only a few hundred dollars more than the Model R.

Like the R, the Model 80 offered the option of an enclosed steel cab, which could come in handy as protection from the elements for a farmer working the tractor to its maximum of 125 acres in one day. With the many outward similarities to the Model R, the 80 was discernible from a distance by its teardrop-shaped flywheel cover and John Deere medallion embedded in the hood above the grille. In just one year's time, 3,500 Model 80 Diesels went out into the field.

Like the 60, the 70 came with 12-volt electrical system and power steering. It also featured an adjustable seat backrest and rack-and-pinion rear-wheel tread adjustment. The 70 had a top speed of 12.5 miles per hour in sixth gear.

The Model 70 Hi-Crop had an adjustable-width front axle. The 70 was available with a gasoline or all-fuel engine initially and had a diesel engine by 1954.

By the time orchard-style Model 60 serial number 6064096 was built on May 1, 1957, Deere's two-digit-series tractors were finished. But as its last all-green two-cylinder tractor shipped off to a destiny unknown, Deere was already building its next legacy.

THE CARDINAL RULES OF TRIPLE DIGITS

Deere's across-the-board replacement of its model numbers, which would go from the tens to hundreds, promised much more to farmers than just a name change. With the introduction of the 20 series came an all-new John Deere tractor, with all-new comfort, all-new power, and all-new precision in the field.

Nearly every aspect of the 20 series, which included the 320, 420, 520, 620, 720, and 820 Diesel models and their variations, was an improvement and advancement in Deere tractors' capabilities. From the two-tone exteriors to the inner workings of the engines, Deere & Company was signaling its leadership in the industry.

These tractors had bigger engines, with improved cylinder heads and pistons to increase horsepower and fuel

Above

A nice feature for operators of the 40C crawler was the hydraulics system for the front blade and attached implements.

Right

The 40C was a quicker machine than its predecessors, capable of 12 miles per hour in fourth gear. A shaft protruding mid track powers the mechanicals used to raise and lower the blade.

Nebraska Test Nos. 503 (1953)/504 (1953 Model 40S)/ 505 (1953 Model 40C)/546 (1955 Model 40S All-Fuel)	
Tractor model	40
Production years	1953–1955
Serial numbers	60001–71814
Drawbar rating (hp)	17.16/16.77/15.11/14.25
Belt pulley/PTO rating (hp)	21.45/21.13/21.24/17.76
Fuel	gasoline (Models 40, 40C, and 1953 40S) and All-Fuel (Models 40H, 40S, 40T-N, 40T-RC, 40T-W, 40U, 40V, and 40W)

The owner of this Model 80 purchased the optional steel cab, which provided protection from the elements and bugs, as well as minimal storage space for food, water, or a few extra tools.

NEBRASKA TEST No. 528 (1954)	
Tractor model	70 Diesel
Production years	1954–1956
Serial numbers	7017500–7043757
Drawbar rating (hp)	34.25
Belt pulley/PTO rating (hp)	43.77
Fuel	diesel (run)/gasoline (start)
The Model 70 Diesel lineup included the 70D (general diesel), 70DH, 70DN, 70DS, and 70DW.	

NEBRASKA TEST No. 567 (1955)	
Tractor model	80 Diesel
Production years	1955–1956
Serial numbers	8000001–8003500
Drawbar rating (hp)	46.32
Belt Pulley/PTO rating (hp)	57.49
Fuel	diesel (run)/gasoline (start)
When the Model 80 Diesel completed the Nebraska Test, it was rated as the most fuel-efficient tractor.	

efficiency. In fact, many of them set Nebraska Test records in low fuel consumption. Hydraulics also were made better and more precise through the incremental settings of Custom Powr-Trol. With these settings, farmers had total control over the pitch of their implements. After the driver lifted an attachment, the memory of the new hydraulic system could return it to exactly the same level of ground work. Additionally, the Deere-exclusive load-and-depth control gave extra traction to the drive wheels under pressure and even raised a potentially mired implement to maintain consistent depth.

Operator seats also were made softer and more buoyant, with an adjustable-tension "rubber torsion spring" supporting each driver's unique body size. This Float-Ride seat sported cushions, a backrest, and optional arm supports. For 50 years, farmers had been adrift in a sea of bumpy, bottom-bruising tractor rides. But with the John Deere 20 series, a farmer truly was a captain of comfort in his craft.

The initial numbered model to make it into its 20s was the new version of the Model 40 crawler, aptly named the 420C. The first 420C actually came off the assembly line the same

day as the first standard model 420, on November 2, 1955. But the crawler had serial number 80002, and the 420S had serial number 80032. Other various included the 420T-RC, a dual-front-wheel tricycle row-crop (RC) tractor with 21-inch clearance, and the 40T-N, a single-wheeled, or narrow, tricycle. Eventually, more than 46,000 of these popular little gems went into the marketplace in 10 different styles.

Like the 420s, the 520s and 620s replaced their 50s and 60s model counterparts. The 620 design was the first to use Deere's hydraulic solution to controlling draft, Custom Powr-Trol. Raising the 620 engine's output to 1,125 rpm from 975 rpm and improving its combustion increased the 620's pull power by 40 percent over its Model 60 foundation. Power steering was standard equipment in the 620 as well as in the 520. The smaller 520 tractor also had more power via increased rpm, plus improved cylinder heads and combustion. The 520 followed its fellow 20-series tractors in its innovative use of hydraulics in the steering column, driver's seat, and hitch assembly.

Deere's switch-hitter, the 720, was incorporated into the lineup as both gasoline and diesel machines. The new row-

NEBRASKA TEST Nos. 599 (1956 Model 420W)/ 600 (1956 Model 420S All-Fuel)/601 (1956 Model 420C)

Tractor model	420
Production years	1956–1958
Serial numbers	80001–136866
Drawbar rating (hp)	20.31/16.42/18.09
Belt pulley/PTO rating (hp)	24.83/19.95/25.26
Fuel	gasoline/All-Fuel

NEBRASKA TEST Nos. 590 (1956 LPG)/592 (1956 All-Fuel)/597 (1956)

Tractor model	520
Production years	1956–1958
Serial numbers	5200000–5213189
Drawbar rating (hp)	25.63/18.58/25.73
Belt Pulley/PTO rating (hp)	32.38/22.62/32.79
Fuel	LPG/All-Fuel/gasoline

NEBRASKA TEST Nos. 591 (1956 LPG)/598 (1956)/604 (1956 All-Fuel)

Tractor model	620
Production years	1956–1960
Serial numbers	6200000–6223247
Drawbar rating (hp)	34.34/33.12/24.50
Belt pulley/PTO rating (hp)	42.79/41.38/30.33
Fuel	LPG/gasoline/All-Fuel

Three variations that Deere & Company built from the general purpose Model 620 design were the 620H, 620-O, and 620S.

crop king, the Model 720 featured the best of Deere's best as standard equipment, including power steering, Custom Powr-Trol implement hydraulics, load-and-depth control hydraulic hitch response, independent PTO, quick-changing adjustable rack-and-pinion rear wheels, front lamps, and a white-and-red warning taillight.

The gasoline, LPG, and tractor-fuel versions of the 720 boasted a dramatically re-engineered motor to increase power and reduce fuel use through decreased displacement,

increased rpm, and improved cylinder heads and pistons. The highest Model 720 power rating went to the LPG engine at 54.2 horsepower on the drawbar and 59.6 horsepower from the PTO or belt. The 720 Diesel cost and weighed a little more than the petrol-tractors, but it sold among farmers. More than a third of the 45,000 row-crop Model 720s built from 1956 to 1958 were diesels.

Least requested of all the heavy hitters in Deere's 20 series was the massive Model 820 Diesel. With a maximum

Cultivating growing crops requires a steady eye and a precise machine. This 1956 Model 420 Hi-Crop sitting astride two rows shows the narrow margin within which operators have to work.

pull of more than four tons, the 820 Diesel produced 69.66 horsepower at the drawbar and 75.60 horsepower from the belt. It had strength enough to pull a 21-foot disk, and by using the optional creeper first gear, it could power a slow-moving pull combine at 1.75 miles per hour. Variations of the 820 Diesel included Rice Special and Industrial models.

Within the 20 series, the only tractor not wholly generated from an older Deere was the Model 320. It had the same look and feel as the other 20 series models, but it represented the smallest standard (320S) and utility (320U) versions of the group. The 2,750-pound 320 never went into a Nebraska Test

because it used the same vertical 4x4-inch engine as the Model 40, originally derived from the Model M. Therefore, it received an unofficial Deere rating as a one- to two-plow tractor. The 320 features included a push-button starter, Touch-O-Matic live hydraulics, and disc brakes, as well as the load-and-depth control three-point hitch. The tractor also had four speeds, and at 22.4 drawbar horsepower and 24.9 horsepower from the belt, it probably pulled more than its own weight, as did the earlier 40. Deere built fewer than 3,100 of the 320s, only 16 of which used all-fuel engines; the rest were gasoline-powered.

NEBRASKA TEST Nos. 593 (1956 LPG)/594 (1956 Diesel)/ 605 (1956)/606 (1956 All-Fuel)

Tractor model	720 and 720 Diesel
Production years	1956–1958
Serial numbers	7200000–7229002
Drawbar rating (hp)	40.63/40.25/39.79/30.97
Belt Pulley/PTO rating (hp)	50.67/50.05/50.25/38.53
Fuel	LPG/diesel (run) and gasoline (start)/gasoline/All-Fuel

Intended for row-crop applications, the Model 720 versions were the 720H, 720N, 720S, and 720W. Model 720 Diesel variations included the 720D (general diesel), 720DH, 720DN, 720DS, and 720DW.

NEBRASKA TEST No. 632 (1957)

Tractor model	820 Diesel
Production years	1956–1958
Serial numbers	8200000–8207078
Drawbar rating (hp)	52.25
Belt pulley/PTO rating (hp)	64.26
Fuel	diesel (run)/gasoline (start)

Deere & Company produced a "Rice Special" version of the Model 820 Diesel because of its massive power and six-speed transmission, which made it capable of pulling a 21-foot disk, multiple drills, or a 24-foot wide cultivator.

THE END OF AN ERA FIRED AT 180 AND 540 DEGREES

By mid-1958, the United States was well into space exploration, sending up Explorer satellites to keep up with the Soviet Union's Sputnik campaign. President Eisenhower had just signed the National Aeronautics and Space Administration into existence and requested $125 million to get the new NASA off the ground.

As the race toward space kept many American eyes looking skyward, Deere & Company was grounded in its effort to make technology advances that would increase the profitability of both the company and its farmer-customers and the plan was working. The company pulled in well more than $470 million, with a profit of almost 9 percent of its sales, firmly planting it among the top 100 of all U.S. manufacturing businesses in 1958. At the same time, the American farmer was faring well. That year, the overall value of U.S. agriculture was $37.9 billion—its second highest up to that point, with crop production alone accounting for more than $15 billion. Farm operators netted their highest take in five years, at nearly $13.2 billion of the agricultural sector's productivity.

Deere's recharged 20 series was still going strong, but it still had room for improvement in the finesse of its tractors. And Deere engineers had designs on the finishing touches for the next and last layer of their historical two-cylinder masterpiece. The 30 series was repackaged with all the mechanical ingenuity of the 20 series plus an outward astuteness for driver comfort, convenience, and safety. The first models of the whole series were built about the same time at both the Dubuque and Waterloo factories in the first week of August 1958. Deere then staggered introduction of the sequenced line, giving local dealerships something new to promote well into 1959. With the help of new Dreyfuss-designed paint and

The 620 was a four-plow tractor, available with gasoline, All-Fuel, and LPG power. The gasoline and LPG models approached 50 belt horse-power. This Hi-crop model is among only 48 produced in that configuration, out of more than 21,000 total 620s that were made. Most were general purpose tractors, though Deere also sold "Standard" and "Orchard" variants.

sheet-metal schemes, farmers immediately picked up on the advanced comfort and other amenities that made these trac-tors plush by the day's standards.

Models 330 and 430 were the smallest of the Deere contemporaries and filled the company's utility market niche

well. The two tractors were similar in overall size, differing only by a couple of inches in width and height on standard versions and by a couple of hundred dollars in price. The distinction to operators, of course, was power. The gasoline-only Model 330 in both its standard and utility forms used the same 4x4-inch vertical two-cylinder as the 320 had. The 430, following suit with its heritage, used the larger 4.25-inch bore in its vertical engine. At an increased rpm output and with a greater compression ratio and displacement, the 430 gained more than 25 percent horsepower at the drawbar over the 330.

In addition to its seven styles and three fuel options, the Model 430 had another unique advantage for a small tractor—a direction-reversal switch that allowed the driver to back up without shifting gears. Labeled as a row-crop tractor, the 430 actually won farmers over as the most all-around utility machine for fieldwork, cleaning stalls, and loading trucks. It sold nearly 14 times more than the Model 330, of which fewer than 1,100 were produced.

For the 30 series, Deere used the same engine groups in their entirety as the 20 series lineup. None of the 30s tractors, with their 20s engines intact, underwent Nebraska Testing because the approval ratings carried over to the new models.

The focus was on the driver's experience of working a John Deere 30-series tractor. Comfort improvements included new operator capabilities, such as climbing on and off the machine more easily using the built-in step and hand grips, sitting with the proper back support on a deeply cushioned, totally adjustable seat, standing up at will on a larger platform, and driving with constant readability of the sloped and lighted instrument panel—which now straddled the steering column—dashboard fashion.

Deere's bigger batch of tractors came from Waterloo, starting with the 530. Still considered an economical tractor for smaller farms, it was not a lesser one. The 530's three interchangeable front-end wheel selections and three-plow capability made it the choice for operations needing a horsepower range in the 30s. More options made this medium-sized tractor into a huge producer, including Deere's Weather Brake cab, which shielded but did not fully enclose the driver, and fender-mounted dual-beam headlights that shone both forward and at the ground flanking the tractor.

As they had with the earlier Deere series, most farmers found more of a need for a larger tractor in day-to-day operations. The Model 630's six speeds made it a versatile fit for jobs ranging from creeper work at 1.5 miles per hour in first gear to 11.5 miles per hour lightweight transport runs in sixth gear. Because the 630 truly gave stronger field performance than the 530, pulling heavier equipment more quickly, it became twice as popular as the 530.

Deere's biggest row-crop tractor in 1957 was the Model 720. Along with the fuels available for the 620, this model also had a diesel-powered version. The 720 made about 57 horsepower at the belt.

The 320V fit into the Deere lineup between the "Standard" and "Hi-Crop" versions. Between 60 and 70 of the Standards (320S) were converted to the 320V configuration, using tires, fenders, drawbar, hitch, and front axles from the 420V. The 320V was also called a Southern Special.

Outselling all of its 30 series counterparts was the giant row-crop machine of the day—the 730. The advancements in Deere's diesel engine made the 730 Diesel a real competitor to its gasoline, all-fuel, and LPG siblings. In 1958, a little less than 2,020 of the ending 720 Diesel tractors were given a direct ignition system, but nearly three-fourths of the 22,000-plus 730 Diesels built had the advantage of a split-load 12- and 24-volt electric start.

Less than a year later, the epitome of two-cylinder power arrived. The last of all Deere's great traction engines: Mr. Mighty, the Model 830 Diesel.

Both weighing in at and pulling more than four tons, the 830 Diesel was the undisputed leader in standard tractor power and equipment capability. Farmers liked its optional foot-pedal accelerator control and choice of V-4 gasoline pony engine or battery-powered electric start. Easily working

The Model 330 was a gasoline-only machine. This 1959 Standard version features a 3-point hitch and yellow seat—not as attractive as black, but a lot cooler when the summer sun's been beating on it. Deere produced just under 1,100 of the Model 330 between 1958 and 1960.

five and six 14-inch bottom plows, 20-foot disks, 21-foot harrows, or a combination of implements, the 830 was Deere & Company's crowning achievement in a two-cylinder diesel.

Variations on its theme led Deere to build hundreds of 840 Industrial Diesel machines during the next two years. In 1959, a small group of the tractors were rebuilt and named New Style 840s, some of which were actually old 820s.

Simultaneously with the 30 series and the 840 industrials, Deere built smaller 435 Diesel and industrial 440 tractors.

The 435 Diesel was the first Deere tractor to have an official drawbar and PTO rating after the Nebraska Tests adopted PTO standards of 540 rpm and 1,000 rpm, thereby doing away with the belt and pulley specifications. In 1959's Test No. 716, the 435 Diesel rated 32.91 PTO horsepower in the 1,000-rpm class.

The industrial 440 used Deere's vertical two-cylinder gasoline or all-fuel engine, unless it was a diesel variation. Both the 435 and 440 diesels used two-cylinders, but they

The flat fenders on this 1959 Model 530 Standard not only held four lights, but also provided a handhold for mounting and dismounting the tractor. The 190-ci engine could be had in gasoline, All-Fuel, and LPG versions, making 34 horsepower at the drawbar with gasoline.

NEBRASKA TEST No. 716 (1959)	
Tractor model	435 Diesel
Production years	1959–1960
Serial numbers	435001–439626
Drawbar rating (hp)	28.41
PTO rating (hp)	32.91
Fuel	diesel
Due to incompatibility among different manufacturers' tractor models and PTO-driven equipment, the farm machine industry adopted standardized PTO speed specifications of 540 and 1,000 rpm in 1958. Hence, the Model 435 Diesel was the first Deere & Company tractor rated for drawbar and PTO-only power.	

weren't Deere engines. The GM two-cycle diesel engine filled the gap with its smaller 3.875x4.5-inch bore and stroke. Interestingly, the first industrial 440 actually was built several months before the first group of the 30 series left production. The two crawler versions of the 440 used five rollers, which was an option starting only with the 430C.

During the last years of the decade, it was obvious that Deere tractors were evolving. Even as its 30 series tractors had quieted the music to farmers' ears with the newly added elliptical muffler, the company was preparing to change its long-held tune about the permanency of its two-cylinder staple.

No one but the top executives knew there was a New Generation of Power waiting to be born. Outwardly, Deere & Company was giving farmers the latest and greatest in mechanical innovations, pushing the engines and ergonomics to the limit. But behind the scenes, the mega-manufacturer had already hurtled over the line of possibility.

The possibility of power in the two-cylinder was tapped. The future of farming required limitless possibility.

On August 29, 1960, Deere & Company officials announced in Dallas that John Deere tractors would meet the future by doing what it had claimed it would never do. The tractor maker would end its era of two-cylinder engines in favor of more cylinders and more power.

The dynamic of Deere's new genesis, although truly powerful and far-reaching, didn't replace America's love of the rugged song sung by Johnny Popper. And with today's growing legions of tractor collectors and club members, sentimental landowners, and hardworking farmers still driving the green-and-golden oldies, it likely never will.

The Model 630's six speeds made it a very versatile machine and able to pull heavier equipment more quickly than the 530. Because of these factors, it became twice as popular as the 530.

Previous pages

The 830 Diesel yielded just under 70 drawbar and 76 belt horsepower, making it Deere's best two-cylinder diesel. The 830 could pull six 14-inch bottom plows, 20-foot disks, 21-foot harrows, and various combinations. Operators liked the foot-operated throttle-and had a long list of options to choose from.

The 30-series models retained the same engines as their 520, 620, and 720 predecessors, but featured improved styling and operator comfort. Among the changes were the oval, low-tone muffler and an improved angle for the steering wheel.

INDEX

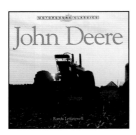

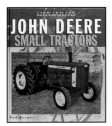
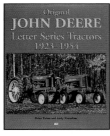
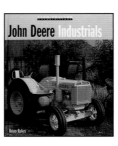

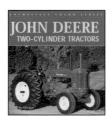